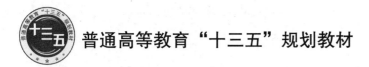 普通高等教育"十三五"规划教材

职场英语写作
——从大学到职场

主编 郝劲梅

 北京邮电大学出版社
www.buptpress.com

内容简介

《职场英语写作——从大学到职场》分为求职和入职两大部分,共七个单元,涉及简历、求职信、面试、商务信函概述、商务书信、电子邮件、备忘录的相关写作。每个单元包括课前活动(Pre-class activities)、介绍(Introduction)、范例(Examples)、写作技巧(Writing skills)和练习实践(Exercises and Practice)五个模块,融职场写作理论、写作技巧与语言学习操练为一体,具有较强的应用性、实践性和职业性。

本书可作为高等院校非英语专业本科和研究生公共英语选修课的教材,也可作为职场新人以及英语水平与此相近的自学者的写作参考书。

图书在版编目(CIP)数据

职场英语写作:从大学到职场 / 郝劲梅主编. -- 北京:北京邮电大学出版社,2019.8
ISBN 978-7-5635-5806-3

Ⅰ.①职… Ⅱ.①郝… Ⅲ.①英语—写作—高等学校—教材 Ⅳ.① H319.36

中国版本图书馆 CIP 数据核字(2019)第 167533 号

书　　　名:	职场英语写作——从大学到职场
主　　　编:	郝劲梅
责 任 编 辑:	廖　娟
出 版 发 行:	北京邮电大学出版社
社　　　址:	北京市海淀区西土城路 10 号 (邮编:100876)
发 　行　 部:	电话:010-62282185　传真:010-62283578
E-mail:	publish@bupt.edu.cn
经　　　销:	各地新华书店
印　　　刷:	北京玺诚印务有限公司
开　　　本:	787 mm×1 092 mm　1/16
印　　　张:	12.5
字　　　数:	299 千字
版　　　次:	2019 年 8 月第 1 版　2019 年 8 月第 1 次印刷

ISBN 978-7-5635-5806-3　　　　　　　　　　　　　　　定价:32.00 元

・ 如有印装质量问题,请与北京邮电大学出版社发行部联系 ・

前言

《职场英语写作——从大学到职场》主要面向高等院校本科生、研究生和职场新人，以提升职场英文书面交际能力为目标，按照大学生从毕业求职到初入职场的顺序展开内容，融职场写作理论、写作技巧与语言学习操练为一体，突出了教材的应用性、实践性和职业性。本书可作为高等院校非英语专业本科和研究生公共英语选修课的教材，也可作为英语水平与此相近的自学者的写作参考书。

全书分为求职和入职两大部分，共七个单元，涉及简历、求职信、面试、商务信函概述、商务书信、电子邮件、备忘录的相关写作。每个单元包括课前活动（Pre-class activities）、介绍（Introduction）、范例（Examples）、写作技巧（Writing skills）和练习实践（Exercises and Practice）五个模块。这五个模块的编排适合教师用于翻转课堂混合式教学，建议教师将前三个模块作为学生课前自主学习的内容，将后两个模块作为课堂精讲、讨论、分析、演示、操练、评价等互动性教学内容。第一个模块针对写作要点和难点，设计探究性学习和案例分析等活动，激发学生对本单元内容的学习兴趣，引导学生开展自主学习，为课堂交流、讨论和实践做准备；第二个模块介绍本单元所涉及的写作体裁结构知识、写作规范等；第三个模块提供典型的写作范例，帮助学生进一步理解写作知识；第四个模块重点介绍写作技巧，配合写作任务，加深学生对写作方法的理解和掌握；第五个模块提供丰富的语言知识练习，帮助学生巩固单元所学内容。

本书主要有以下特色。

- **启发性、思辨性：** 本书着重培养学生在职场英语写作中的分析、对比、归纳、总结、质疑等思辨能力，设计的课前活动和写作任务能引导学生积极主动地思考、探讨、分享，发现问题，解决问题。

- **实用性、操作性：** 针对学生求职就业的需求及写作中的要点难点，将案例讨论、语篇程式、范例分析、写作策略技巧、语言学习操练、改错互评等写作活动有机结合，内容丰富，写作任务和练习操作性强。

- **系统性、连贯性：** 本书各单元以及每个单元的各部分内容彼此关联，前后贯通，由浅入深，层层递进，从多角度多维度提供深入透彻的讲解和操练，体现出教材设计的系统性和内在逻辑性，有利于学生对职场写作的理解、掌握、巩固和运用。

- **直观性、趣味性：** 本书配有大量的样文图表，并将两位虚拟人物——刚毕业的学生 Sarah Jones 和计算机专业在读研究生林风的职场发展和相应的写作实践贯穿全书，清晰明了，生动直观地讲解了职场英语的写作要领和方法策略，便于理解和记忆。

由于编者知识水平有限，错误与不当之处在所难免，敬请读者批评指正。

编者
2019 年 8 月

Contents 目 录

PART ONE: FINDING A JOB

Unit 1 Resumes ·· 003
  I   Pre-class activities ··· 003
  II Introduction ··· 009
  III Resume examples ·· 016
  IV Writing skills ·· 022
  V   Exercises and Practice ··· 027

Unit 2 Cover Letters ·· 038
  I   Pre-class activities ··· 038
  II Introduction ··· 041
  III Cover letter examples ·· 046
  IV Writing skills ·· 051
  V   Exercises and Practice ··· 056

Unit 3 Job Interviews ·· 061
  I   Pre-class activities ··· 061
  II Introduction ··· 063
  III Sample interview questions and answers ························ 071
  IV Interview skills ·· 074
  V   Exercises and Practice ··· 078

PART TWO: STARTING A JOB

Unit 4 Workplace correspondence: Overview ················ 085
 Ⅰ Pre-class activities ················ 085
 Ⅱ Introduction ················ 088
 Ⅲ Writing skills ················ 095
 Ⅳ Exercises and Practice ················ 101

Unit 5 Professional Letters ················ 106
 Ⅰ Pre-class activities ················ 106
 Ⅱ Introduction ················ 107
 Ⅲ Letter Examples ················ 113
 Ⅳ Writing skills ················ 118
 Ⅴ Exercises and Practice ················ 122

Unit 6 Professional E-mails ················ 132
 Ⅰ Pre-class activities ················ 132
 Ⅱ Introduction ················ 134
 Ⅲ E-mail Examples ················ 139
 Ⅳ Writing skills ················ 144
 Ⅴ Exercises and Practice ················ 151

Unit 7 Professional Memos ················ 161
 Ⅰ Pre-class activities ················ 161
 Ⅱ Introduction ················ 162
 Ⅲ Resume examples ················ 166
 Ⅳ Writing skills ················ 171
 Ⅴ Exercises and Practice ················ 174

Answer Key ················ 181

Reference ················ 191

PART ONE
FINDING A JOB

Unit 1 Resumes

> Resume writing is an important life skill in today's fast-changing workplace. Knowing how to write a clear, effective and professional-looking resume is key to a successful job search. This unit takes you through the steps of creating a job-winning resume that accurately reflects your skills, experience, and educational background. You will study different types of resumes, sections of a resume and resume formats. You will also learn to use specific tips and techniques to tailor your resume for a specific job.

Objectives

After completing this unit, you will be able to

◆ Research the job and yourself before the application writing;
◆ Understand the differences among reverse chronological, functional and combination resumes;
◆ Identify the components of a resume and arrange these components effectively;
◆ Understand and apply the techniques for targeted resume writing;
◆ Use effective language and key words in your resume.

 I Pre-class activities

Research and Explore

Task 1. Do preliminary research on the following questions and get prepared for class discussion.

(1) What is the purpose of a resume?

_____

_____

(2) What kind of resume can grab the attention of a recruiter or an employer within seconds?
_____
_____

Task 2. Research the job / position that interests you.

Before you write a resume, you usually need to do some research on the job. Search for job advertisements that match your education and experience from online job sites, newspapers, company websites, and college and university websites. Go through each one and identify the keywords that the company uses to describe the job requirements and job responsibilities. Make a list of the keywords common to these ads. Bring one of the job ads to class, share the list of keywords with your peers and discuss how to incorporate those keywords into your resume to impress the employer.

Task 3. Research yourself.

Researching yourself helps you find the job that is right for you. Make a list of the needs of the prospective employer based on the job ads you browsed in Task 2. Write statements about your relevant qualifications detailing how you used that skill or exhibited that quality and pointing to any positive results or accomplishments. Complete the following table about job requirements and your qualifications.

Job title: _____

Job description (Keywords)	My qualifications
Education / Knowledge	Highest level of education: Relevant knowledge / courses / training: Overall academic performance:
Experience	Relevant experience (summer job, part-time job, internship, project, volunteer, extra-curricular activities, community service, etc.) 1.　　　2.　　　3.
Responsibilities	My major responsibilities in each of those areas: The key skills I used or gained in that job: Impressive results or accomplishments of that particular job (quantify them in numerical or other specific terms):

Unit 1   Resumes

(Continued)

Job description (Keywords)	My qualifications
Skills	Technical skills: Language skills: Transferrable skills (leadership, communication, organization, time management, teamwork, etc.) gained through your academic study and / or related work experiences. (Refer to the Experience Section for evidence) :
Personal characteristics	My general personality / work-related personality:

Task 4. Search for resumes.

Team up with other students in the class who major in the same field as you. Conduct an online search for resources which provide resumes. Find a job category that is the closest to your major. Collect at least three resumes (it's preferable to find different types of resumes). Discuss the differences between those resumes, the techniques for creating an effective resume, and your resume writing problems.

Task 5. Draft your resume.

With your knowledge of the job and resume writing, write the first draft of your resume in response to the job ad that interests you in Task 2. Bring your resume to class for peer review.

☞ See "Introduction" in Section Ⅱ and "Resume examples" in Section Ⅲ for help.

📢 Case study

Task 6. Lin Feng (林风) is a second-year postgraduate student majoring in computer science in a Chinese university. He has a strong academic record and extensive research and project experience in college. He is interested in a software engineer intern position posted on LinkedIn (see the job posting below). Look at his resume and answer the following questions:

(1) Does this resume match the job seeker's education, experience, and skills to the job requirements listed in the posting?

(2) What format and language mistakes does this resume make?

☞ See "Resume Sections" in Section Ⅱ for help.

(3) How should the job seeker use power words to highlight his strengths and employability?

Job Description

The qualified candidate will join Intel China Flex Services - Platform Software Technology team as a software engineer intern. He / she will have opportunities to participate into various projects as part of product development or research. The work will mainly focus on system level software areas such as OS kernel, BIOS / Firmware development, network / graphics or other I / O driver development, imaging / media development, etc.. And the good performer will have high opportunity to join Intel China after graduation.

Qualifications

- Postgraduate students in Computer Science, Computer Engineering or Electrical Engineering
- Must be comfortable with working in a fast-paced environment
- Proficient in C and / or C++
- Proficient in programming and / or debugging and / or troubleshooting skills in system level software development
- AI and visual computing knowledge and experience are plus

Soft skills

- Strong self-learning capability in different technical areas
- Fluent spoken and written English would be a plus
- Communication skills with internal or external partners, customers and vendors would be an advantage

Lin Feng's original resume:

Resume

LIN FENG Age: 24
, Xueyuan Road, Haidian District, Beijing, 1000 Health: Excellent
Home: (010)-****-**** | Cell: 186******** Marital Status: Single
E-mail: linfeng9999@163.com Hometown: Chengdu

(Continued)

Education	
Master of Science in Computer Science, ABC University, Beijing	Anticipated 05 / 2019
Bachelor of Science in Computer Science, ABC University, Beijing	05 / 2016
1st place: ABC University Debugging Contest (Spring 2015)	

Technical Skills

Languages: Java, C, C++, SQL, Python

Operating Systems: Windows, Unix, Linux

Database Systems: Access, SQL Server, MySQL, Oracle

Internships	
Software Engineering Intern, **ABC Company**, Beijing	03 / 2017 – now
• Help to develop an application of a new customer account system	
Programming Intern, **XYZ Company**, Beijing	06 / 2016 – 09 / 2016
• Maintenance and testing of the applications	
• Solved the problems	
• Was praised and recognized by colleagues	

Academic Projects	
Mobile Application: Edu-Life Studio, ABC University	02 / 2017 – 05 / 2017
• In charge of the design and development of mobile apps	
Campus Web Application, ABC University	9 / 2015 – 12 / 2015
• Maintained and developed campus web applications	
Internal Purchasing Systems Development, ABC University	10 / 2014 – 12 / 2014
• Participated in the creation of a purchasing system	

☞ Compare this original version with the revised one (Resume examples #1) in Section Ⅲ.

Task 7. Sarah Jones is a recent graduate from California State University with a bachelor's degree in political science. She wants to apply for the position of office manager advertised in a local newspaper (see the job ad below). However, she has limited relevant experience required for the position, and the job is not closely related to her major. Examine the resume she wrote.

(1) Are the facts listed in the resume relevant to the position and able to impress the employer? What information could be eliminated or provided to make her background and experience more relevant to the position? What information should be prioritized or focused?

(2) Is the resume layout visually appealing to the reader?

```
┌─────────────────────────────────────────────────────┐
│                  JOB OPPORTUNITY                     │
│  Corefact Corporation is looking for responsible     │
│  team-oriented person for                            │
│                   OFFICE MANAGER                     │
│  Duties & Responsibilities:                          │
│  • → Perform general as well as specific             │
│       administrative duties including office         │
│       management.                                    │
│  • → Prepare and proofread letters, emails, memos,   │
│       proposals, etc.                                │
│  • → Arrange training for staff                      │
│  • → Assist the HR manager on HR matters             │
│  • → Update and ensure the compliance of office      │
│       procedures                                     │
│  Job requirements                                    │
│  • → Strong communication and interpersonal skills   │
│  • → Good computer & software skills                 │
│  • → Excellent organizational skills and attention   │
│       to detail, with the ability to multi-task      │
│  • → Ability to work in a fast-paced environment     │
│  DEADLINE: June 20, 2016                             │
│  Email your CV along with application letter to:     │
│  corefact-career@gmail.com                           │
│       Only shortlisted candidate will be contacted   │
└─────────────────────────────────────────────────────┘
```

Sarah Jones' original resume:

Sarah Jones

sarahjones@yahoo.com　5555 Hemlock St, Sacramento, CA 95841　Home: +(916) 498-5555　Cell: (256)555-5555

Education:

　Bachelor of Arts in Political Science, May 2017

　California State University, Sacramento, CA

Experience:

　Agway Inc., Sacramento, CA　June 2015, 2016

　As Office Intern, I was responsible for performing office duties and providing support to various department; wrote letters, emails, memos, and reports as assigned.

　Nelmar Construction Inc, Fair Oaks, CA　July 2015

　As assistant, I was responsible for processing files and purchasing office supplies.

　Dion's Warehouse, Sacramento, CA　January 2015, Salesperson

　Whitney High School　March 2012 – May 2013, Editor-in-chief of School Paper

Hobbies:

　Tennis, sailing, travel, music, and gardening

☞ Compare this original version with the revised one (Resume example #2) in Section Ⅲ.

II Introduction

A resume provides a summary of your skills, abilities and accomplishments with the intent to motivate an employer to interview you. A great resume has the ability to persuade a prospective employer that you have the unique talent and experience desired and that you deserve a personal interview for the position. So, when you write a resume, don't forget that you should sell your skills and accomplishments, not just list your work history and personal information.

Resume vs. Curriculum Vitae (CV)

Both resumes and CVs are used in job application, but there are some differences between them.

Resume	Curriculum Vitae
More concise; usually 1~2 pages	Longer and more detailed; 2 or more pages
Present a brief, targeted list of skills and qualifications for a specific position	Present a full record of your career history (academic background, teaching experience, honors, research, awards, publications, presentations, grants, and other achievements)
Used when applying for a non-academic position in industry, non-profit, private and public sector	Used when applying for an academic, scientific or medical position at a college, university, or research institution
Mainly used in the US and Canada where CV and resume are sometimes used interchangeably	Used in Europe, the Middle East, and Africa where CV is used in all contexts and resumes aren't used at all
Include categories like Contact Information, Education, and Experience	In addition to categories like Education and Experience, a CV can contain other categories: Publications, Presentations & Lectures, Professional Associations, Research Interests, Teaching Experience, Research Experience, Licensure Grants, etc.

Resume Sections

A standard resume should include the following basic sections:
- Contact Information
- Experience Section
- Education Section
- Skills Section

Additional sections can be included when they best represent your qualifications for the position:

• Resume Summary or Resume Objective

• Activities

• Honors and Awards

• Hobbies and Interests…

Be sure to choose unique resume sections that best reflect your qualifications instead of adding every possible section to your resume.

Here is the order of resume sections for college students:

• Contact Information

• Objective

• Education

• Experience / Internships

• Extra-Curricular Activities (Leadership)

• Skills

• Hobbies and Interests

Sections	Information to include	Tips & Examples
Heading / Contact information 个人信息	• full name • complete mailing address • phone number(s) • E-mail address	• Appear at the top of the resume • Name should be in bold print and the largest font size • May include both a campus and a residential address • Use a professional E-mail address. Avoid an unprofessional E-mail address like tutifruti92@hotmail.com ◇ Should **NOT** include personal information like age, gender, height, weight, health condition, hometown, religion, and marital status **Cameo Bohnino** Campus Address:　　　　Permanent Address: 227 Harrison, Apt. 5　　　5226 Buckbridge West Lafayette, IN 47906　Fort Wayne, IN 4681 765.410.6283　　　　　　260.482.670 E-mail: cbohnino@purdue.edu Cell: 765.410.6283

(Continued)

Sections	Information to include	Tips & Examples
Objective (additional) 求职意向	• the position you want • career field or industry you want to work in • company name (if applicable) • key skills you plan to use in the position	• Be specific. Avoid writing objective that is too general and vague *(e.g. a challenging position that offers room for advancement)* • Focus on what you can bring to the job, not what you want **OBJECTIVE** 　　To obtain the position of Operations Manager for ABC Company where my extensive skills and background in management and customer service may be best applied to achieve ABC's operational goals
Qualifications summary / Profile (additional) 资历摘要	most impressive skills, abilities, and accomplishments that are relevant to the position • number of years of experience • relevant education, certifications, special training • key accomplishments very broadly stated • key strength, skills, abilities or characteristics for the position	• A 3~4 sentence paragraph or bullet-point list, up near the top • The main goal is to immediately grab the hiring manager's attention and share your most impressive qualifications up front • Tailored to the job posting **QUALIFICATIONS SUMMARY** • Internship experience using newest accounting computer programs • A.A.S. degree with honors in accounting • President of student accounting club – initiated speakers program • Demonstrated ability in organizing, follow-through to the last detail • Committed to producing results above and beyond what's expected **PROFILE** 　　Over five years of sales, customer service, and management experience. Skilled in project coordination, time management and the ability to work with a team to achieve department objectives. Proficient in several computer software programs including MS Office.

(Continued)

Sections	Information to include	Tips & Examples
Education 教育背景/学历	• name of school, location (city and state or province) • major and minor • degree earned or seeking • (i.e. BS, BS, MS, MA, PhD) • graduation date or expected graduation date (month / year) • GPA (if above 3.0) • relevant coursework • (if this adds strength to your resume) • class rank (if you rank high in class) • study abroad programs • academic honors, scholarships • special project or senior thesis topic	• List the highest degree first in reverse chronological order • List it above EXPERIENCE section if you are still in school or you are just completing your education, or if it holds the greatest proof of your qualifications for the position • If your education is a trump card, list it twice; once in your summary, and once again in its own section • Relevant course work may be listed separately as a subsection under Education • Academic honors may be listed in a separate section if there are many of them **EDUCATION** **Master of Business Administration** (Expected May 2012) Fuqua School of Business, Duke University, Durham, NC GPA: 3.5 / 4.0 **Bachelor of Science**, magna cum laude (2009) University of Texas, Austin, TX Major: Mechanical Engineering Minor: Mathematics GPA: 3.8 / 4.0
Experience 工作经历	• the positions held / jobs title • company name, location • dates of employment • skills, responsibilities and accomplishments	• May include any **relevant experience**: paid or unpaid work, full time or part time work, internship, volunteer, project, leadership, etc. • Use **active verbs** (developed, planned, organized, etc.) • Use **bullet lists** to describe each position but be consistent • Stress the major **responsibilities and results / achievements** • Use present tense for present events (e.g. Supervise) and use past tense for past events (e.g. Supervised) • Complete sentences containing "I" are rarely used • Consider creating specific experience sections to highlight different types of experience, such as "Internship Experience" "Project / Research Experience" "Leadership Experience" etc. • Use the same **keywords** as in the job requirements

(Continued)

Sections	Information to include	Tips & Examples
Experience 工作经历	• the positions held / jobs title • company name, location • dates of employment • skills, responsibilities and accomplishments	**EXPERIENCE** **Assistant Manager**, XYZ Restaurant St. Paul, MN May 2013—present • Supervise staff of sixteen including cooks, waiters, and hostesses • Track and order weekly inventory equaling more than $ 2 000 in merchandise • Experienced a 98 percent customer-experience success rate when addressing customer complaints or problems **Summer Intern** ABC Communications, Houston, TX June 2011—August 2011 • Partnered with design intern to create and execute two sell sheets, one print ad., and one postcard • Created and presented collaborative intern campaign to entire agency and founders of organization • Awarded best campaign of competing teams
Activities / Extracurricular activities / Volunteer (additional) 活动经历 / 社会实践	• position title, organization name, location • dates of your involvement	• May choose to include a description of your campus activities, leadership positions, memberships in clubs or student organizations, volunteer experience, community service experiences depending on whether or not the experience can showcase employer desired skills • May use the same format as EXPERIENCE section
		EXTRACURRICULAR ACTIVITIES **Member**, Union College Badminton Club, Schenectady, NY September 2016 – Present **Treasurer**, New School of Northern Virginia Drama Club, Fairfax, VA September 2013 – June 2015
Research / Projects (additional) 研究经历 / 项目经历	• project name • organization name • year of the project • roles, responsibilities, achievements	Include in your resume if they might contribute to your employability. May use the same format as EXPERIENCE section.
		ENGINEERING PROJECTS **Senior Capstone Project: Robotics Design**, Union College, Schenectady, NY, Fall 2015 • Collaborated with team members to design and assemble a stepper motor powered vehicle that picked up ping pong balls and dropped them into three separate holes ranging from seven to ten feet apart • Programmed all aspects of the vehicle to travel via remote control in every direction using MATLAB

(Continued)

Sections	Information to include	Tips & Examples
Skills 技能	Computer / Technical skills • level • certificate • languages, software, hardware, etc. Language skills • foreign language level, certificate	• Include all the required skills as many as possible • Use the same keywords in the job advert • State your proficiency level with languages and programs *(fluent, advanced, proficient, intermediate, basic, exposure to, etc.)* **TECHNICAL SKILLS** 　Proficient in C++, MATLAB, SolidWorks Microsoft SharePoint, Project, Word, Excel and PowerPoint 　Familiar with Electronics Work Bench, PSpice and Java **LANGUAGE SKILLS** 　Fluent in French, Intermediate Mandarin, and conversational Japanese
Honors & Awards (additional) 荣誉与奖励	academic honors • scholarships, honor • awards won for specific activities or subjects work-related honors	Don't include them if they have zero to do with work or don't show you in a professional light. **AWARDS** 　Dean's list - UCLA, Spring 2014 　Tech Valley Business Plan Competition, *Semifinalist* April 2015 　Union College Business Plan Competition, *First Prize* January 2015 　USA Snowboard Association National Championships, *Bronze Medal Winner* Winter 2013
Interests (additional) 兴趣爱好	hobbies, interests, talents	Only include those that are unique, specific, and / or relevant to the job. **HOBBIES & INTERESTS** 　Creative writing. Member of the Active Travelers Club. Reading on the latest trends in the organic industry.

Resume layout / format

Categories	Tips
Length 长度	• 1 page for undergraduate students and recent grads. Fill the page completely. Include as many key words as possible to increase the likelihood that your resume will be selected in a keyword search • 2 pages may be acceptable for grad students and others with extensive relevant experience. ◇ Only print on **one side of the paper**, and your second page should include your name and page number in a footer from page 2 onwards

(Continued)

Categories	Tips
Font size & style 字体	• Use 10~12 point size in formal, professional and readable fonts (Times New Roman, **Arial**, **Verdana**, Cambria, Calibri, Georgia, **Tahoma**, Garamond, etc.). Try a slightly larger font for headings and name. • Use **bold type**, *italics,* and CAPITALIZATION to highlight key areas such as your name and major section headings. ◇ Whatever font styles you choose, be consistent.
Bullet point 项目符号	Experience descriptions should be in bullet list format. Use • or ■. Avoid dashes, arrows, check boxes, or diamonds. ◇ Use parallel structure for similar items.
Spacing & margins 间距与页边距	Use white space between sections of your resume to make it easy to read. Adjust the margins to fit your content. 1-inch margins are typical, but not a strict requirement.
Paper size & color 纸张	2 standard paper sizes, depending on the part of the world: • A4 (297×210 millimeters) — used largely in China, Europe, including the United Kingdom • US Letter Size (8 1/2×11 inches) — used largely in the United States.
	White, cream, and ivory are acceptable color for resume and cover letter. ◇ Use bond paper (24# weight is suggested). ◇ Use the same paper for your letter.

Resume Guidelines

Relevant

• Only include the points that are relevant to the job posting. Tailor your resume to the employer. Avoid needless information.

Concise

• Use phrases or short statements; do not use sentences. Use bullets, not paragraphs when describing your work experience.

Consistent

• List information in a consistent way.
• Use one typeface (boldface, underlining, and italics) consistently throughout your resume.
• Keep the formatting and verb tenses to be consistent throughout.

Correct

• Make sure your resume is error free. Eliminate typos and grammatical errors.

Appealing visually

• Make your resume clear and easy-to-read.

III Resume examples

The following are typical resumes with comments on the writing techniques and characteristics. These are not intended to be the examples of the perfect resume. Use them as a guide to assist you in writing more informative, persuasive, and professional resumes.

1. A master candidate (Science) with relevant experience writes a chronological resume for IT internship.

Below is a reverse chronological resume of a Computer Science major emphasizing his relevant technical skills and experience. It is the revised version of Lin Feng's resume which contains mistakes and problems in formatting and phrasing. Compare two versions and identify the changes in this resume.

Lin Feng's resume (revised version)

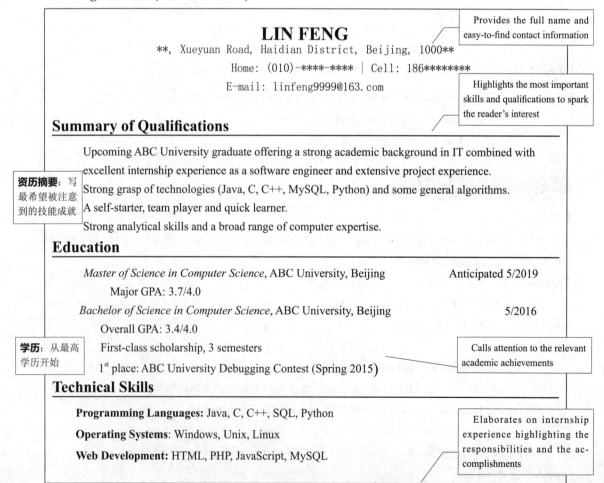

Internships

Software Engineering Intern, ABC Company, Beijing   3/2017 – Present

- Provide coding support for the software network of the 100-employee company, improving the reliability and efficiency of core systems.
- Team up with senior software engineers and architects to create a new customer account application using C++ and Java. The application is eventually used by more than 50 000 users.

Programming Intern, XYZ Company, Beijing   6/2016 – 9/2016

- Updated and maintained the existing software and databases.
- Troubleshot web application performance problems.
- Provided online and desk support to the end users and responded to their queries.
- Received award for outstanding service as an intern.

> 实习经历：由近至远列举相关经历

> Uses more powerful action verbs such as "provide" "improve" "create" "update", etc.

Academic Projects

Lead developer, Mobile Application: Edu-Life Studio, ABC University   2/2017 – 5/2017

Led a 4-person team to develop a personal education and entertainment mobile app that has achieved up to 10K downloads with 4+ average rating.

Co-developer, Campus Web Application, ABC University   9/2015 – 12/2015

Collaborated with a team of 3 peers to update, maintained and developed web applications for various departments at the university including admissions, financial services and student records; increased unique views from 90 per month to 500 per month.

Programmer, Internal Purchasing Systems Development, ABC University   10/2014 – 12/2014

Assisted in the creation of a shared purchasing system to retrieve data and provide online processing of purchasing requests by departments and university functions.

> 实习经历：由近至远列举相关经历

> Provides quantifiable results such as "10K downloads" and "4+ average rating" "increased unique views from 90 to 500"

2. A fresh graduate (Political Science) writes a functional resume for the post of office manager.

Below is a functional resume which emphasizes the applicant's relevant skills and experience. It is the revised version of Sarah Jones' resume. Compare the format and style of two versions and discuss the advantages and disadvantages of a functional resume.

Sarah Jones

sarahjones@yahoo.com   5555 Hemlock St, Sacramento, CA 95841   Home: +(916) 498-5555   Cell: (256)555-5555

> The typeface is easy on the eyes Name is larger and bold

OBJECTIVE

To secure the position of office manager in a fast-paced business environment.

PERSONAL PROFILE

A dynamic and responsible individual with experience in providing full secretarial, administrative and office management support to work in a busy office environment. Excel in interacting with people at all levels of the organization. Good written and oral communication skills. Advanced computer skills in MS Office Suite and other applications / systems.

> 求职目标：说明求职的职位及对工作环境的期待

> Uses **bold font** and all CAPS to highlight section headings

> 个人概述：突出能胜任职位的各种技能

RELEVANT SKILLS

Administration

- Provided full secretarial and administrative support to the 10-person marketing department for Agway.
- Increased office efficiency by 20% by developing efficiency-enhancing workflow.
- Scheduled meetings, appointments; arranged two marketing events for Agway.
- Performed filing and data management for Agway and Nelmar Construction.
- Managed purchase of office supplies for Nelmar Construction.

HR and Training

- Organized human resources management workshop for new staff for Agway.
- Coordinated staff training and professional development workshops for Agway and Nelmar Construction.
- Assisted the HR manager in hiring new staff for Agway.

Writing

- Drafted and edited all official correspondence and weekly production reports for Agway. Reduced inaccuracies and provided management with an important decision-making tool.
- Turned CEO ideas into written proposals to increase office productivity in Agway.
- Created customer documentation and financial statement for Nelmar Constructions.

(Annotation: Focuses on three most relevant and marketable skills for prospective employer)

(Annotation: Uses bullet points to list duties and accomplishments, making it easier to read)

(相关技能：挑选个人最强的工作技能，列举承担的工作职责和成绩)

EMPLOYMENT

Office Intern, Agway Inc., Sacramento, CA Summer 2011, 2010
Administrative Support Intern, Nelmar Construction Inc, Fair Oaks, CA Summer 2009

(就业经历：工作时间不长，一笔带过)

EDUCATION

California State University, Sacramento, CA
- Bachelor of Arts in Political Science, May 2012
- Additional courses and training in business management, accounting, human resources office management, and business law

(Annotation: Education section is listed near the end of the resume when the degree is unrelated to the current position)

(学历：写最高学历；专业和工作不太相关，但额外的课程和培训与职位相关)

CAMPUS ACTIVITIES

Managing Editor, Whitney High School Paper, Sept. 2008 – May 2009
- Wrote columns and editorials, and edited articles.
- Hired and oversaw associate and assistant editors.

(校园社团活动：与工作相关)

3. PhD candidate (Science) writes a two-page resume for a generalist position with a management consulting firm.

Below is a detailed resume written for a firm which allows a two-page resume and is looking for strong academic achievement. The candidate showcases his GRE scores, undergraduate GPA, awards, and publications in journals, demonstrates research experience, leadership experience, and analytical / quantitative skills.

Abi Demir
54 Dunster Street • Cambridge, MA 02138, USA • 617-555-5555 •xxx@harvard.edu

EDUCATION

Harvard University — Boston, MA
Ph.D. candidate in Biological and Biomedical Science — Expected May 2017
GRE: 800Q, 610V, 5.5W, 99% BIOCHEM

Nanyang Technological University — Singapore
B.S. with First Class Honors in Biological Science. GPA: 3.96/4.00 — May 2011
Minor in Entrepreneurship

University of Melbourne — Melbourne, Australia
International Student Exchange Program — Feb – Jul 2011

RESEARCH EXPERIENCE

Harvard Medical School — Boston, MA
Graduate Researcher — 2012 – Present
- Designed and executed novel biochemical experiments to test epigenetic inheritance of silent chromatin in budding yeast
- Developed protocol for and mentored 3 postdocs on nucleosome reconstitution
- Developed thermodynamic model to analyze electromobility supershift assays
- Performed statistical analysis on data sets using Excel and Prism Graphpad
- Collaborated with postdocs, a structure biology lab in Germany, and simulation scientists from Denmark and Australia

Nanyang Technological University — Singapore
Research Associate — 2009 – 2011
- Managed and negotiated ordering for lab consumables, equipment, and services. Assisted in lab maintenance and organization
- Initiated, designed, and executed 2 independent projects, studying aggregation behavior of nucleosome core particles (NCP), and the self-assembly of NCP-liposome complexes
- Performed statistical analysis on data sets using Origin
- Mentored and trained 2 graduate students

LEADERSHIP / TEAMWORK EXPERIENCE

Harvard Office of Technology Development — Boston, MA
Fellow of Early Technology Assessment — Jan 2016 – Present
- Analysed potential applications for 4 cases of new technologies from the Harvard biomedical community
- Performed prior art search to facilitate IP development
- Evaluated potential market to project the size and value of new biotechnologies
- Performed competitor analysis by investigating companies with related products on the market or in pipelines
- Evaluated challenges to facilitate strategy development
- Identified companies with necessary expertise and resources to bring technologies to market

Harvard Biotech Club — Boston, MA
Director of Internal Affairs — 2015 – Present
- Worked in team of 10 to organize the Harvard Biotech Club annual Career Fair, attracting 20+ companies and ~ 650 job seekers
- Recruited and mentored new director of the club

Director of IT and Communications — 2014 – 2015
- Established and maintained relationship with ~50 companies / institutions seeking to advertise events / job openings
- Managed the biweekly club bulletin which has 2500+ members
- Designed and maintained the club website using FrontPage, KompoZer and Cyberduck
- Mentored the succeeding director of IT on listserv management and website design

Abi Demir   617-555-5555   Page 2/2

Harvard Division of Medical Sciences Patent Law Path   Boston, MA
Co-Leader   2014 – Present
- Initiated and organized biennial Patent Law Info Course, resulting in 100+ applicants each year, expanded from 4 weeks in 2012 to 7 weeks in 2014
- Organized patent law career transition panel discussions in 2015, featuring 5 panelists and attracting 100 + attendees

Harvard Graduate Women in Science and Engineering (HGWISE)   Boston, MA
Department Representative   2013 – 2014
- Organized "HGWISE McKinsey Women in Consulting Fireside Chat" in team of 6. Wrote a 600-word news report, published on the HGWISE website

Harvard Medical School   Boston, MA
Teaching Assistant   Fall 2014
- Selected as teaching assistant for Principle of Genetics, 1 of 3 core courses for the graduate program
- Designed and led weekly lecture review and discussion sections for group of 11 students
- Graded student assignments, met with students, and maintained a course web site

Harvard Division of Medical Sciences Bulletin   Boston, MA
Editor   2012 – 2014
- Developed and planned content for the quarterly bulletin in a team of 5 editors
- Contributed 3 articles to the bulletin

ADDITIONAL EXPERIENCE

Mini-MBA course by Harvard Graduate School of Arts and Sciences Business Club   Boston, MA
Participant   2013
- Exposed to basic concepts in business through intensive five-week courses based on *The 10-Day MBA* by Steven Silbiger
- Actively participated in case discussions led by faculty from Harvard Business School or leading industry professionals

SKILLS

Language:
English – Full professional proficiency
Chinese – Native or bilingual proficiency

PUBLICATIONS

- **A Demir** and D Moazed. *In preparation*. Sir3 cooperative binding to chromatin conferred by its C-terminal winged helix dimerization domain mediates silent chromatin assembly in *S. cerevisiea*.
- F Wang, G Li, **A Demir**, MA Currie, A Johnson, D Moazed (2015). "Heterochromatin protein Sir3 induces contacts between the amino terminus of histone H4 and nucleosomal DNA." *Proc Natl Acad Sci USA* 110(21): 8495-8500.
- NV Berezhnoy, D Lundberg, N Korolev, **A Demir,** J Yan, M Miguel, B Lindman, L Nordenskiold (2014). "Supramolecular organization in self-assembly of chromatin and cationic lipid bilayers is controlled by membrane charge density." *Biomacromolecules* 13(12):4146-4157.
- Y Liu, **A Demir,** Y Yang, YP Fan, N Korolev, L Nordenskiöld (2013). "Influence of histone tails and H4 tail acetylations on nucleosome-nucleosome interactions." *J Mol Biol* 414(5): 749-764.
- D Lundberg, NV Berezhnoy, **A Demir**, N Korolev, CJ Su, V Alfredsson, MG Miguel, B Lindman and L Nordenskiold (2012). "Interactions between cationic lipid bilayers and model chromatin." *Langmuir* 26 (15): 12488-12492.

4. An experienced IT professional with impressive work experience writes a resume for IT Manager position.

Below is a resume designed with a creative template. The unusual layout helps the information to stand out well while still maintaining a professional and organized look.

Scott Jackson

IT Manager

Personal Info

Address
970 Drummond Street
Newark, NJ 07102
USA

Phone
202 555 0177

E-mail
Scott.w.jackson@gmail.com

WWW
futureisnow.scottjackson.com

LinkedIn
Linkedin.com/scott-jackson

Twitter
twitter.com/scottjacksonofficial

Additional Skills

Adobe Photoshop
Excellent

InDesign
Excellent

CRM Platforms
Proficient

Google Analytics
Proficient

Google AdWords
Advanced

Languages

Spanish
C1

German
B2

Skills Summary

Programming and App Development
- Developed and built 20+ mobile Apps and 30+ websites providing exceptional user experience.
- 15+ years experience in C/C++, Cocoa, and Objective-C.
- C Certified Professional Programmer (2006), C++ Certified Professional Programmer (2009).

Leadership
- 8+ years experience in team management (teams of 10~50 colleagues) and project coordination.
- Designed and implemented a new IT management model with Apple's New York Branch, increasing the quarterly productivity by 33% and resulting in increase in employee statistics.
- Trained and mentored 50+ junior developers for certification exams (88% success rate).

Business management
- Coordinated 20+ projects with a budget over $200 000.
- Optimized procurement processes to reduce BCD M%E's annual costs by 27%.
- Successfully cooperated with sales and marketing teams on new business strategies which helped increase Apple New York's sales volume by 27%.

Experience

IT Manager   2012-03 – Present
Apple, New York City, NJ
- Supervised the IT team in creating mobile apps providing the best user experience for Apple's customers all over the world.
- Developed, reviewed, and tested innovative and visionary new applications using emerging technologies.
- Guided talent that provides technical support and training while working in partnership with the business team.

Senior IT Specialist   2006-08 – 2012-02
BCD M&E, New York City, NJ
- Developed, reviewed, and tested websites for internal and external stakeholders, led innovation in mobile applications.
- Cooperated with procurement teams in optimizing procurement processes.

Programmer   2002-09 – 2005-12
Oracle, Redwood City, CA

Education

MS in Computer Science, Distinction   2001-09 – 2002-06
The City College of New York, New York City, NJ

BS in Computer Science
University of California, Berkeley, CA   1997-09 – 2001-06

IV Writing skills

Choosing the most appropriate resume type

There are three main types of resumes, namely, reverse chronological, functional and combination. The first consideration when writing a resume is to choose the right resume type depending on your personal situation and the optimal strategy to best highlight your strengths and achievements. The table below describes each type and provides the guides for choosing the resume type. Use it to decide which is best for you.

Resume Type	When to choose it
Chronological Resume (Job-based)（倒序型简历 / 工作简历） • Listing education and work history in reverse chronological order with the most recent first, followed by the previous. • Easier to read and write. • The most traditional, popular and preferred style.	(1) You have a consistent or solid work history without job hopping or lapses. (2) You want to show your career progression, especially if you are hoping to move up. (3) You want to highlight current responsibilities and educational credentials. (4) You are looking for a job in the same or similar fields. (5) You are applying to a traditional or conservative employer.
Functional Resume (Skill-based)（功能型简历） • Focusing on skills and experience and de-emphasizing work history. • Grouping a variety of experiences around skill categories followed by work history section in reverse chronological order without outlining the duties. (See resume example #2 in Section Ⅲ)	(6) Your job history is not consistent or successive (such as employment gap, changing jobs), but you have the skills relevant to the position. (7) You want to highlight your skills and abilities desired by the employer or to demonstrate transferrable skills acquired through unpaid activities. (8) You have little or no work experience. (9) You want to emphasize your future potential while downplaying your limited or irrelevant education or credentials.
Combination (Mixed)（综合型简历） • Listing your skills first and then detailing education, employment history and education. • Blending the flexibility and strength of the other two types of resumes, highlighting both your skills and traits and providing a chronological listing of your work experience.	(10) You want to present not only your skills and experience but also the career growth. (11) You desire a job change in a related career field. (12) Your previous work experience is unrelated to your current career path and you want to promote your top marketable skills. (13) You are a recent graduate but have a solid work history that is unrelated to your area of study.

Unit 1 Resumes

Your Name	Your Name	Your Name
Street Address City, State, Zip code Phone number Email address **Work Experience** Company Name, Dates of employment • Job title, description, responsibilities Company Name, Dates of employment • Job title, description, responsibilities Company Name, Dates of employment • Job title, description, responsibilities **Education** • School name -City, Date of attendance Degree, Major, Related coursework **Skills/Awards** • Computer, language or other personal skills • Computer, language or other personal skills	Street Address City, State, Zip code Phone number Email address **Professional Skills** MANAGEMENT _____ SALES _____ COMMUNICATION _____ LEADERSHIP _____ **Work history** • Job title, Company name, Dates • Job title, Company name, Dates **Education** • Degree, Major, Date earned, School name	Street Address City, State, Zip code Phone number Email address **Qualifications** _____ **Key Skills** _____ **Relevant Experience** Company Name, Dates of employment • Job title, description, responsibilities Company Name, Dates of employment • Job title, description, responsibilities **Education** • School name -City, Date of attendance Degree, Major, Related coursework
Chronological resume	Functional resume	Combination resume

Task 8. Read the sample resumes in Section Ⅲ. Identify the type of each resume and the possible reasons for choosing the resume type. Review the situations (1~13) listed in the table above and write down the number of the situation that apply. And then determine what is the best type for your resume.

                        Resume type   Reasons for choosing it

Lin Feng's resume: _____   _____

Sarah Jones' resume: _____   _____

Abi Demir's resume: _____   _____

Scott Jackson's resume: _____   _____

Your resume: _____   _____

Writing a targeted resume

    It's critical to write a resume tailor-made for a specific employment goal in a job search. A targeted resume tailors your skills and experiences to match the desired skills listed in a job posting. It is likely to convince the employer your work will benefit the company and that you should be among the candidates to be interviewed.

1. Include the keywords from job descriptions.

    The easiest way to customize your resume is to embed the keywords from the job advertisement. You can extract different types of keywords from different sections of a job posting and use them when referring to job titles, accomplishments, experience, skills, education, career objectives and training. That way, the hiring manager and applicant tracking system will detect the keywords in your resume when screening candidates for job openings.

> **TIP: Keywords** are position-related expressions which describe experience, skills, and traits, words that an employer looks for in a candidate. They are necessary to get HR managers' attention and pass the screening software for online job applications.
> **Types of Keywords for Resumes**
> **Education**—BA, MS, MBA, and PhD
> **Job Titles**—UX Designer, Business Development Manager, and Full stack Developer
> **Industry—Specific Skills**—Bookkeeping, product launch, and proposal writing
> **Soft Skills**—Problem solving, communication, sales, and team management
> **Training and Certification**—Six Sigma, Project Management, and ITIL
> **Industry Jargon**—Asset management, A/B Editing, and digital video editing workflow
> **Impressive Terms**—Fortune 500 and top salesman.

Task 9. Read the following job advertisement and the resume. Underline the keywords in the job posting and match them with the same keywords or the synonyms of keywords in the resume.

(Job advertisement-Office manager)

JOB OPPORTUNITY

Corefact Corporation is looking for responsible team-oriented person for

OFFICE MANAGER

Duties & Responsibilities:
- Perform general as well as specific administrative duties including office management
- Prepare and proofread letters, emails, memos, proposals, etc.
- Arrange training for staff
- Assists the HR manager on HR matters
- Update and ensure the compliance of office procedures

Job requirements:
- Strong communication and interpersonal skills
- Good computer & software skills
- Excellent organizational skills and attention to detail, with the ability to multi-task
- Ability to work in a fast-paced environment

(Targeted resume)

EMELDA LOPEZ

PERSONAL PROFILE
Energetic and team-oriented Office Manager skilled at working with a diverse group of people. Strong organization, communication, and interpersonal skills. Eager to bring administrative skills to a growing company and work in a fast-paced office environment.

HILIGHTS
- Documentation
- Scheduling
- Staff training
- Executive management support
- Business correspondence
- Computer proficiency
- Database administration

EXPERIENCE
Office Manager   08/2008 to Current
Signa Architects, New Cityland, CA
- Supervise large administrative staff focused on design and construction support.
- Assist with Human Resources duties including new hire packets.
- Schedule meetings, appointments; and executive travel.
- Write and edit business letters, emails, memos, and reports.

Office Manager   09/2004 to 07/2008
Foundation for Economic Growth, New Cityland, CA
- Performed filing and data management
- Coordinated with outside vendors on supplies.
- Oversaw office staff and trained new employees.

2. Include a Summary of Qualifications, Profile or Career Highlights section.

A Summary of Qualifications or Profile, usually put at the top of a resume, is a brief summary of an applicant's most impressive skills, experiences, and goals as they relate to a specific job opening. The purpose is to spark the hiring manager's interest and increase your chances of getting a job interview. You can create such a summary and tailor it to meet specific job requirements as listed in the job posting. A Summary of Qualifications or Profile usually lists the following things:

• A general overview of your role within your current or previous organization followed by the amount of relevant experience

• Major skills / qualities you can bring to the new company with a highlight of your impressive achievements or awards

• An example of your ability the company needs

• Relevant classes or certifications you've achieved

• Interests / Passions / Personality traits relevant to the job

• Your career objective

Summary of Qualifications or Profile can be bulleted or written as a short paragraph (no more than six sentences).

e.g.

Summary of Qualifications: Inquisitive computer science specialist with 8+ years of experience. Looking to leverage strong programming skills as a developer for Google. Led a team of 11 coders at Halcyon-Berth Systems. Delivered projects an average of 10% before deadline, with 15% less errors than other teams. Trained 25 programmers in cloud computing skills.

Profile
• 2.5 years as Marketing Coordinator for mid-size communications firm producing flyers, newspaper advertisements, brochures, and online content.
• BA in Marketing and Communications from University of Michigan (2009).
• 2 years' blogging experience promoting and reviewing on-campus social events.
• Committed to building expertise in web communications, social media, and search engine marketing through exceptional work ethic and ability to quickly absorb and apply new information.

☞ Finish Task 12, 13 in "Exercises and Practice" section.

3. Prioritize the information and use more targeted headings for a specific position.

The recruiter's task is to find a candidate that is best suited to their vacancy. So you need to prioritize your resume from recruiter's perspective.

• Present what is of greatest interest to your potential employer first.

• Prioritize your qualifications and accomplishments by importance or relevance to the job you're applying for if you have many jobs or experiences.

• Use targeted headings for a specific position in order to make the resume more relevant to the job.

For example, if you are applying for a teaching position, use the heading "Teaching Experience" instead of "Experience" and put this section before other experience sections, such as research experience, volunteer or community involvement, leadership roles you have held in the community or in a student organization.

Task 10. Look at the following table. For each position, change the order of the content to emphasize the relevant experience. Pay attention to the targeted headline for a specific job

	Position to apply for	Content to include	Prioritize the content
1	Event Coordinator position, responsible for servicing events	(1) Campus activities (2) Customer service experience (3) Event planning experience	
2	Supply Chain Executive position, responsible for improving operations and providing leadership	(1) Sales accomplishment (2) Logistics management accomplishment (3) Consulting accomplishment	
3	Higher education administration position responsible for directing and overseeing the daily administration of the school	Core competencies: (1) Degree & Program Management (2) Public & Community Relations (3) Student Engagement & Development	

Using compelling and strong power words

Hiring managers are tired of vague and cliched words like "make" "good" "hard worker" "successfully" or meaningless words like "responsible for" and "duties included" in job candidates' resumes. So, it is important to use dynamic, vivid and compelling words that make you stand out. You should:

(1) Use **strong action verbs** that define specific experience, skills, and accomplishments in previous roles, such as design, accomplished, and initiated. The following are the best terms that hiring managers would like to see on a resume.

The Best Resume Terms

① Achieved: 52%
② Improved: 48%
③ Trained / mentored: 47%
④ Managed: 44%
⑤ Created: 43%
⑥ Resolved: 40%
⑦ Volunteered: 35%
⑧ Influenced: 29%
⑨ Increased / Decreased: 28%
⑩ Negotiated: 25%
⑪ Launched: 24%
⑫ Won: 13%

(Source: Hiring Managers Rank Best and Worst Words to Use in a Resume in New CareerBuilder Survey | CareerBuilder, http://www.careerbuilder.com)

(2) Use **concrete examples, numbers and quantifiable statements** to make your past accomplishments more impressive and credible. For example, Lin Feng does a better job using action verbs coupled with quantifiable statements to describe his internship experience and highlight his accomplishments.

Before	After
• In charge of design and development of mobile apps. • Developed and maintained campus web applications. • Was praised and recognized by colleagues.	• Led a 4-person team to develop a personal education and entertainment mobile app that has achieved up to 30K downloads with 4+ average rating. • Collaborated with a team of 3 peers to develop and maintain web applications for two departments at the university including admissions, financial services and student records; increased unique page views from 90 per month to 500 per month. • Received award for outstanding service as an intern.

☞ Finish Task 15, 16 in "Exercises and Practice" section.

V Exercises and Practice

Writing the Summary of qualifications / Profile

Task 11. Complete the following statements with the appropriate prepositions. (in, of, at, with, for, to, about, as)

(1) Recent honor graduate _____ a BA _____ Advertising, looking _____ an entry-level position _____ Business Management or Sales.

(2) Over 10 years' extensive experience _____ the legal profession _____ a strong background _____ civil litigation, excellent interpersonal skills and the ability _____ communicate effectively.

(3) A dynamic team leader; able _____ prioritize, delegate tasks, and make sound decisions quickly, seeking an opportunity to work _____ a Product Manager _____ an IT company.

(4) Proven ability _____ multi-task under pressure and coordinate _____ external agencies.

(5) Able to provide employers _____ administrative support and professional communications skills.

(6) Possess excellent leadership skills. Capable _____ adapting to changing work environment.

(7) Proficient _____ Microsoft Word, Access and Excel.

(8) Dedicated _____ creating inclusive classrooms and introducing innovative learning activities for students.

(9) Adept _____ producing high-quality deliverables.

(10) Strong passion _____ the interior design industry.

(11) Passionate _____ data security and natural language processing.

(12) Known _____ an interactive teaching style that encourages student participation.

Task 12. Use the expressions about the applicant's education, skills, experience and achievements to create a Profile for your resume.

Adj. (trait /quality)	N. (role / job title)	N. (experience / skills / qualities)	V. (action / achievements)
• motivated • energetic • efficient • dedicated • organized • accomplished • experienced • adaptable • flexible • resourceful • ambitious • diligent • highly skilled • hard working • reliable • dependable • dynamic • enthusiastic • results-oriented • detail-oriented • target-driven	• Physics major • junior History major • final year IT undergraduate • Master of Business Administration • recent graduate • Finance & investment graduate • upcoming graduate • honors student • Research Associate • Marketing student assistant • professional • entry-level mechanical engineer	• ___ years of experience in / as • extensive / hands-on / broad experience in / from • strong / extensive background in • strong / proven ability to • proven track record of • analytical / communication / interpersonal / negotiation / language / computer / technology skills • strong/solid / good / expert / in-depth / comprehensive knowledge of • strong awareness of • keen / genuine interest in • genuine love / passion for • leadership and academic training at • demonstrated skills in • accomplishment in • initiative • self-motivation • out-going personality • willingness to work hard	• meet deadlines and objectives • meet and exceed goals • assume additional responsibilities • acquire knowledge quickly • build highly motivated teams • handle multiple tasks • work under pressure • work with diverse personalities and different cultures • work well independently as well as collaboratively in a team setting • lead and supervise subordinates effectively • collect and analyze information and quickly grasp what needs to be done • manage and complete projects efficiently / to the highest standards • think outside the box in identifying problems • adapt quickly to any situations • ensure a down-to-earth approach

Profile:

Writing the Education Section

Task 13. Use the following words or phrases to complete the Education Section.

Major, Minor, Bachelor, Master, Expected, Concentration, Rank
Overall, Thesis, Double, Honors, Senior Project, Relevant Courses

Unit 1 Resumes

> **List your highest level of education first**, then work your way backward. Include your GPA only if it is higher than 3.0.

(1)

Education
Stanford University
_____graduation date: May 2019
• Bachelor of Science in Biology
• _____: Economics
• _____ GPA: 3.2 Major GPA: 3.8

(2)

Education
Columbia University   *May 2016*
_____ of Science, Technology Management
New York University   *May 2014*
_____ of Arts: Marketing

(3)

Education
BS, Computer Science
_____: Software Engineering
Peking University
GPA: 3.5/4 _____: 9/320
Honors each semester

(4)

Education	M.S. in Geography	Washington University, St. Louis MO
	2009	_____: "Geographies of military bases and their surrounding communities"
	B.A.	Washington University, St. Louis MO
	2005	_____ major: Geography and Sociology

(5)

ABC UNIVERSITY- Sometown, NH
Bachelor of Science in Information Technology   2011
• Honors: Graduated cum laude (GPA: 3.53); Dean's List, 2009, 2010, 2011.
• _____: Enterprise Application Development, Security, Java / C / VB Programming, IT Project Management, Database Programming, Web Design, Computer Architecture.
• _____: Obtaining Grade A on capstone project as co-developer of Web-based, customized enterprise software solution that integrated business processes for a nonprofit organization. Delivered turnkey application that reduced manual data entry, saving hundreds of personnel hours monthly.

Writing the Work Experience Section: Using action verbs to describe job responsibilities

Task 14. Choose the appropriate verbs to fill in the blanks. Change the word form if necessary.

> **Action verbs** help keep your descriptions short and powerful. Avoid using the first-person pronoun "I" and unparallel structure.

Research / Technical

[*analyze, author, conduct, create, develop, identify, resolve, provide, research, troubleshoot*]

(1) _____ dynamic, high-speed websites, apps and platforms.
(2) _____ needs analyses, usability tests and feasibility studies.
(3) _____ and implemented algorithms using C++ and MATLAB programs.

(4) Interpreted and _____ quantitative and qualitative results related to the Good Parenting Project.

(5) _____ problems with the LAN and maintained network infrastructures.

(6) _____ prompt technical support for 120 clients.

(7) _____ a paper for publication in *Organic Chemistry*.

Management / Leadership / Supervision

[coordinate, establish, manage, motivate, organize, resolve, spearhead, delegate, initiate]

(1) Established a nine-member productivity team and _____ operational tasks to three junior managers.

(2) Prioritize and _____ multiple projects within specifications and budget restrictions.

(3) _____ project efforts between mechanical designers, engineers and project managers.

(4) _____ human resources management workshops for new staff.

(5) _____ teammates and resolved conflicts among fellow team members.

(6) _____ a two-year national campaign to promote green business.

Communication / People / Writing

[communicate, deal, negotiate, present, promote, write, correspond, persuaded, maintain]

(1) Established and _____ relationships with local and regional employees.

(2) _____ with customers in a courteous, pleasant and professional manner.

(3) Served as company liaison to _____ business relations with clients and potential vendors.

(4) _____ favorable rates and terms for software licenses, office supplies.

(5) _____ research findings at the National Conference on Ecotourism.

Supporting / Helping

[assist, collaborate, participate]

(1) _____ with the interdisciplinary team to construct an engaging on-air program.

(2) _____ recruiters and HR managers with human resources functions.

(3) _____ in group meetings and discussions pertaining to the research project and suggested ideas for club improvement.

Achievements / Results / Recognition

[achieve, earn, exceed, increase, reduce, receive, win, result in, rank, outperform, award]

(1) Accomplished the stated goals, _____ production goals by 35%.

(2) _____ customer satisfaction by 23% annually.

(3) _____ record-high ratings on customer satisfaction surveys.

(4) _____ a reputation for maintaining a positive attitude and producing high-quality work.

(5) _____ contracts totaling over $20 M/year in new revenue.

(6) _____ "Volunteer of the Year" award for contributions to morale and efficiency.

(7) _____ in the top 3 amongst all wait staff at multiple venues for the highest ticket averages.

(8) Restructured program for purchasing department supplies, which _____ 28% cost reduction.

(9) _____ Employee of the Month Award on five separate occasions for exceeding sales quotas.

(10) _____ peers in constructing online reports with Infocast.

Writing the Experience Section: Emphasizing results and accomplishments

Task 16. Improve the following vague and weak statements on a resume by using this formula:

> **Work experience** section should be specific and reflect your **results and accomplishments**. It is not a list of duties.

Action Word + Details + Results / Accomplishments = Power Sentence

Consider using gerund, attributive clause, preposition for achievements statements and quantifying results or accomplishments.

Restructured claims approval process, which decreased processing time by 20%.

Saved the organization $6,000 using thorough data analysis and system upgrades.

Planned and coordinated numerous marketing events, resulting in a significant increase in new members.

e.g.

Weak: Responsible for writing user guides.
(Hints: How many user guides? For how many people? What was the result?)

Better: Wrote six user guides for 15 000 users two weeks before deadline.

Weak	Better
(1) In charge of major projects. (Hints: What kind of projects? What was the result?)	(1) _____
(2) Duties included testing various applications. (Hints: What kind of applications? What was the result of testing?)	(2) _____
(3) A good team player in college speech and debate team. (Hints: What did you do specifically? What awards or prizes did your team win?)	(3) _____
(4) Led a sales team. (Hints: How many people? What were the specific duties? What were the team's achievements?)	(4) _____
(5) Organized activities and engaged students. (Hints: What activities are organized? For whom or how many? Through what media? What was the result?)	(5) _____

Writing the Experience and Activities sections: Including job title, date, organization and experiences.

Task 17. Covert the following paragraphs into bulleted lists and put them after the

right headings. **Be sure to include the date, job title and use the correct tense and parallel structure.**

> **Tense:** Use the past tense for past experiences and the present tense for current experiences.
> **Parallelism:** Use the same part of speech when you describe your jobs. It is best to use verbs. Don't mix nouns and verbs. Parallelism makes your resume easier to read and understand.

(1) In addition to my academic training in international studies, I also have extensive internship experience in research and analysis support. From 2015 to 2017, I was a Research Intern for the Washington Institute for Near East Policy. By collaborating with 3 interns, I collected data, performed research, and authored reports for interviews and publications on subjects including Arab Politics, NGOs in Egypt and Tunisia. In addition, I monitored key regional political developments.

(2) Since July 2016 I have been employed as a Software Engineer by I-Solution, where I am responsible for maintaining and developing high quality software systems for clients and utilizing software engineering tools to perform technical root cause analysis.

(3) Outside the classroom I am involved in playing soccer for the Salisbury University soccer team. Currently I am responsible for motivating 20 players and coordinating all indoor practices as well as scheduling all weight room activities. As the Captain, it is my responsibility to set a standard of excellence through hard work and dedication.

(4) From 2013 to 2015, I worked as a System Analyst at ABC Company. I performed feasibility studies, data modeling and analysis service and implemented decision support system for the Real Estate Division.

Section	Description
Work Experience	2016 — Present 2013—2015
Internship	
Activities	

Writing the Skills Section

A separate Skills Section may be pulled out to highlight those skills that are especially relevant to the position, such as computer skills, lab skills, or design skills. You can use adjectives to describe your technical or language skills and achievements.

Task 18. Translate the underlined expressions into Chinese.
Computer skills:

<u>Proficient in</u> C++ and MATLAB _____

<u>Experienced in</u> Adobe Photoshop, Illustrator, and Sketch _____

Expert knowledge of databases: Oracle and Microsoft SQL 2000 / 2005 _____
Basic knowledge of Visio, Adobe Acrobat, and Photoshop _____
Working knowledge of Microsoft Office Suite _____

Language skills:

CET-6 (530/710), TOEFL (105) Proficient in reading, writing, and speaking English
Mandarin (Native), English (Fluent), Japanese (Conversational), Spanish (Beginner)
Advanced writing level in English and Intermediate speaking level in Spanish

_____ _____ _____ _____ _____ _____ _____

Certificates:

First-level Certificate for National Computer _____
Microsoft Certified IT Professional _____
Microsoft Certified Technology Specialist _____
Certificate of Accounting Professional _____
Certified Public Accountant _____

Writing the Honors & Awards Section

Include this section if you have too many relevant honors to list outside of education. You can add a statement about the award to highlight your achievements. e.g. The Samsung Scholarship (awarded to top 3% students).

Task 19. Match the following honors and awards with their English equivalents.

国家励志奖学金	Outstanding Graduate
一等奖学金	Advanced Individual / Outstanding Student
三好学生	Excellent Student Cadre
先进个人	First-Class Scholarship
优秀学生干部	Honor Student / Merit Student / Straight A Student
优秀毕业生	National Encouragement Scholarship
"外研社杯" 英语演讲大赛	ABU Asia-Pacific Robot Contest
全国英语演讲比赛	China College Students' Innovation and Entrepreneurship Competition
第十七届全国大学生英语辩论赛	Contemporary Undergraduate Mathematical Contest in Modeling
全国英语风采大赛	National English Talent Competition for College Students
全国大学数学建模竞赛	The 17th National English Debate Competition for College Students
全国大学生电子设计竞赛	National Undergraduate Electronic Design Contest
国际大学生程序设计竞赛	Business Plan Competition
亚太大学生机器人大赛	"FLTRP Cup" English Public Speaking Contest
中国大学生创业计划竞赛	International Collegiate Programming Contest
创业计划大赛	National English Speaking Competition

特等奖	Meritorious Winner / First Prize Winner
决赛选手 / 特等奖提名	Successful Participant
半决赛选手	1st Place / 2nd Place / 3rd Place
一等奖	Gold / Silver / Bronze Medal Winner
金牌 / 银牌 / 铜牌	Outstanding Winner
荣誉奖 / 优秀奖 / 鼓励奖	Honorable Mention
成功参赛奖	Finalist
第一名 / 第二名 / 第三名	Semifinalist

Task 20. Edit and revise. Correct the errors in the following sections of resumes.

(1) Heading

Resume

Name: Li Ming	School: BUPT
Address: No. 10 West Tucheng Road In Haidian District in Beijing	Born: June, 1985
	Gender: Male
Phone: 134××××××××	Marital status: Single
E-mail: Ming-Li@163.com	Excellent Health

(format, irrelevant personal information)

(2) Education

- **Bachelor of Science in Communication Engineering**   June 2012
  Harbin Engineering University
- **Graduate of Science in Communication Engineering**   June 2015
  Beijing University of Posts and Telecommunications
  Main Course:
  Communication Theory, Signal and System, Wavelet Analysis, C++ Language

(organization, grammar, punctuation)

(3) Experience

RELATED EXPERIENCE
Salesperson   *Walmart, Shenzhen*   September 2014 to present
• Merchandise displays
• Managed and tracked inventory
• Maintaining customer relationships
Shift Supervisor   May 2013 to August 2014
Star Coffee Shop, Shenzhen
• Train 5 new employees
• Handle total sales

(consistency, parallelism, tense)

_____
_____
_____
_____

(4) Honors and Awards

Rewards:
First-prize Scholarship （two times）
Three-Good Student Reward 2009.11
The Top Place in Liaoning Province in National Undergraduate Electronic Design Contest in 2011

(wording, layout)

_____
_____
_____
_____

(5) Activities

September 2010 — May 2011 I worked as a volunteer for my neighborhood. I worked as a network assistant. assembled 20 computers for my friends and neighbors, loaded software on each one, and networked them.

(format, "I")

_____
_____
_____
_____

(6) Skills

> LANGUAGE LEVEL
>   Past CET-6, can read write, listen and speak.
> COMPUTER LEVEL
>   Familiar with the operation of MS Word, Excel, PowerPoint effectively, know of C, C++, grasp Java, Linux, basic understanding of Dreamweaver, Adobe Photoshop and so on.

(consistency, wording)

_____

_____

_____

Assignments

1. Find 2~3 resumes of your classmates. Use the following checklist to review and critique the resumes. Share your comments with the author when you are finished.

2. Use the resume checklist to revise the first draft of your resume.

Resume checklist

SECTIONS
• **Remove unnecessary items** Delete personal information like religion, marital status, ethnicity, age, gender or hometown. If you're in college or a recent graduate, structure your resume like this: Name, Contact Information, Education, Work Experience, Leadership / Extra-curricular Activities, Additional Info (Skills, Languages, Interests) • **Name & Contact Details**   Include your full name, Address (Street Address, City, State, Zip code), phone number (Home and Cell), E-mail Address. • **Education** Include all colleges you've attended, along with the type of degree you received, your major, minor and graduation year. Start with your highest degree first. Include your GPA if it's above 3.0 out of 40. • **Work Experience / Internship** Use reverse chronological order for your jobs. Your current or most recent job should appear first. Include your company name, positions held, dates worked, plus a short description where necessary. Use action words (e.g. developed, managed, etc.) to describe your specific responsibilities in present or past tense. Focus on your accomplishments and quantify your accomplishments by using numbers wherever possible. Organize your bullets by importance and relevance. • **Projects, Extra-curricular, Leadership or Volunteering Experiences (optional)** Include university projects, extra-curricular or leadership experiences that are relevant to your role. • **Additional Information (optional)** Include languages, technical skills, professional societies / memberships or interests.

(Continued)

LAYOUT / FORMATTING

- **Visually pleasing & easy to read**

Use bullets, bolding, lines to guide the readers' eyes through the document and highlight important content.

Be consistent in your use of bold, italics, underlines, capitalization, date formats, font sizes, bullets, alignment and spacing.

Use professional font styles. Use a font size between 10~12. No more than two standard font styles.

Information is not too crowded on the page.

Keep your resume to one page if you have less than 10 years of experience or at most two pages.

Upload it in PDF format

LANGUAGE

- Use clear and strong action verbs to describe experience and achievements.
- No grammatical, punctuation, spelling, and typographical errors.
- Current job is in present tense while past jobs are in past tense.
- No "I" statements.
- No inappropriate abbreviations and jargons.

STRATEGY

- Tailor your resume based on the industry and company.
- Include keywords to get past resume screening software.

Unit 2　　Cover Letters

The power of a cover letter in job application should never be underestimated. A well-written cover letter reveals your work ethic, attention to detail and your personality that a resume can't. To ensure that your resume is read by the employer, you will need a cover letter that markets your unique qualifications for the specific job requirements. In this unit, you will study types of cover letters, sections of a cover letter and cover letter formats. You will also examine the ways to enhance your cover letter and learn about techniques to successfully "sell" yourself to prospective employers.

Objectives

After completing this unit, you will be able to
◆ Identify the parts and features of a cover letter;
◆ Explain how to apply the AIDA organizational approach to a cover letter;
◆ Understand how to develop a persuasive cover letter to accompany a resume;
◆ Produce an attention-getting opening paragraph and persuasive body paragraphs;
◆ Use effective language in your cover letter.

I　Pre-class activities

Research and Explore

Task 1. Do preliminary research on the following questions and get prepared for class discussion.

Your job application writing consists of a cover letter and a resume. However, there has been a debate about whether cover letters still have a place in recruitment, or indeed, whether employers actually read them.

(1) How can you write an eye-catching cover letter that will set you apart from the rest?

_____
_____
_____

(2) Why is a cover letter needed when you have a resume ready? What's the relationship between a cover letter and a resume? What should be highlighted in a cover letter? What can't be put into a resume but can be included in a cover letter?

_____
_____
_____

Task 2. Research the organization.

In Unit 1, you have conducted research on a particular position and yourself. Continue your research and preparation in job application by focusing on a prospective employer. This employer may be the company in the job advertisement you've found or a particular organization you would like to work for after graduation. Research this employer utilizing a variety of sources such as the company's web site, press about the company, current or former employee references, etc..

• Find the details about the company that motivate you to apply: mission or philosophy, reputation, history or background, strategies and goals, areas of specialization, services or products, new projects, etc..

• Be prepared to explain whether the organization is right for you and how you will incorporate the knowledge of the employer into your cover letter.

Task 3. Draft your cover letter.

Review the job advertisement you've found and your own resume. Answer two questions before writing: Why are you interested in the job or this employer? Why should the employer be interested in you? Write down 2~3 reasons why you are a good candidate for the position or why you want to work there. Consider how your skills and strengths can contribute to the company. Draft a cover letter of more than 200 words specifically targeted to the position you apply for and bring your draft to class for peer review.

☞ See Section Ⅱ and Section Ⅲ for help.

🔊 Case study

Task 4. Lin Feng writes a general cover letter to accompany his resume. The cover letter, however, is unlikely to get the recruiter's attention or win him a job interview. Discuss in groups the mistakes or problems this cover letter has.

Please think from an employer's perspective.

> Dear Sir or Madam,
>
> Thank you very much for looking through my cover letter and I sincerely hope to receive your support and recognition. My name is Lin Feng. I am writing to apply for the Software Engineer position posted on LinkedIn.com. because the position sounds exactly like the kind of job I am seeking.
>
> I major in Software Engineering. I am pursuing master's degree at ABC University. During my undergraduate education, I studied hard and earned excellent results. I have been awarded scholarships for many times. I have the great interest in computer technology. I have grasped the principals of my major and skills of practice. Not only have I passed CET-6, but more important I can communicate with others freely in English. My ability to write and speak English is out of question.
>
> As for my experience, from March 2017 to now, I am an intern at ABC Company responsible for creating a new customer account system. From June 2016 to September 2016, I was a software engineer intern at XYZ Company where I developed and tested applications. I participated in three projects. The first one is Mobile Application of Whole Note Studios, the second is Internal Purchasing Systems Development, and the last is Campus Web Application.
>
> I believe I am qualified for this position and look forward to joining your company. Thank you very much for considering my application. I hope to hear from you soon.
>
> Sincerely,
>
> Lin Feng

☞ Compare this cover letter with the revised version in Section Ⅲ.

Task 5. Sarah Jones submits her cover letter along with her resume via email as requested in the job posting. In this case, she attaches her cover letter and resume and then writes a brief email cover letter that pulls from the first and last paragraph of her formal cover letter. Read the following email cover letter and discuss with your peers the following questions:

(1) Is the subject line clear and effective? Can you improve it?

(2) Why does she write a short email cover letter first instead of copying and pasting the original version of her cover letter into the email message directly? What's the function of this short email cover letter?

> From: Sarah Jones sarahjones@yahoo.com   Sent: June 5, 2016
> To: corefact-career@gmail.com
> Subject: Sarah Jones' cover letter and resume
> Attachments: SarahJones CoverLetter.pdf
>   SarahJones Resume.pdf

(Continued)

Dear Ms. Castro:

I am applying for the position of Office Manager at Corefact, which I saw posted recently on dayjob.com. I'm extremely enthusiastic about this opportunity and believe I am well qualified. My relevant experience as office intern and administrative assistant has demonstrated my strong administrative, communication and interpersonal skills.

Attached are my cover letter and resume for your review. I can be contacted either through e-mail or by calling (###) ###-####. I look forward to hearing from you. Thank you for your consideration.

Sincerely,
Sarah Jones

☞ Compare this email cover letter with the original longer version in Section Ⅲ and find their differences.

II Introduction

A cover letter is a document sent with your resume to provide additional information on your skills and experience. Its main purpose is to advertise your strengths and assets in a way that would interest employers in interviewing you. A well-written one can give you the edge you need to secure an interview in today's competitive market, while a poorly written letter will likely disqualify you.

Keep in mind that your cover letter should complement and add value to your resume, and therefore do not just copy and paste the information from your resume into your cover letter. In the cover letter, you can highlight specific information from your resume, show your enthusiasm and personality, and add more explanations about your hard skills and soft skills.

Types of cover letters

Ad-response letter / solicited cover letter / application letter（应聘求职信）
This type of letter is written when you are responding to an advertised job opening. It matches your qualifications to the position requirements.

Letter of interest / cold-contact letter / unsolicited cover letter / prospecting letter（自荐求职信）
You use this type of letter to contact employers who have not advertised job openings to introduce yourself with the hope that it may spark the employer's interest and result in a job interview.

Hard-copy cover letter （打印版求职信）

Your cover letter may be a printed out hard copy. Hard-copy cover letters are similar to email cover letters in content but have different formatting, especially in terms of address and contact information.

E-mail cover letter （电子版求职信）

It is more common to submit your job application materials via email or through job websites. When emailing your cover letter, it's important to follow the employer's instructions on how to send your job application documents.

Parts of a Cover Letter

A cover letter consists of several parts: contact information, a salutation, the body of the cover letter, a closing, and a signature. The body section includes 3~4 paragraphs which usually use a technique called **AIDA**. It is short for **Attention, Interest, Desire and Action**. A cover letter needs to be direct, short and well written. Make sure it emphasizes your suitability for the job.

1. Hard-copy cover letter

A cover letter can be broken down into the following sections:

Parts		Information to include	Examples
Header	Your Contact Info.	Address City, State, Zip Code Phone Number E-mail	222 Morewood Ave. Pittsburgh, PA 15212 (414) 555-9999 jgoodman@gmail.com
	Date	Current date	April 16, 2014
	Employer Contact Info.	Name of HR Manager or Recruiter Job Title Company Name Company Address City, State, Zip Code	Ms. Judith Castro, Director Human Resources Natural History Museum 1201 S. Figueroa St. Los Angeles, CA 90015
Salutation		A greeting (Whenever possible, address to a specific person or hiring manager. Phone or email to get the recipient's name and title. If you can't get a name, use a title such as "Dear Director" "To Whom it May Concern" or "Dear Sir or Madam")	√ Dear Mr. / Ms. / Dr. / Professor[LAST NAME] √ Dear [FIRST & LAST NAME] √ Dear HR Manager / Hiring Manager √ Dear Recruiting Department × Dear Mrs. LAST NAME 　(not professional because there is no way of determining someone's marital status)

(Continued)

Parts	Information to include	Examples
Opening paragraph **Grab the Attention — A 抓住注意力**	• Why you are writing *(the specific job you are applying for)* • How you heard about the job *(ad in a specific place for a specific person or a particular person's suggestion)* • How you are qualified for the job / How you would benefit the company *(Briefly highlight your 2~3 key skills, which will add value to the employer. Also, look at the job posting, it will typically tell you the skills required.)*	*Your company recently advertised on the dayjob.com website for a Studio Assistant. After reading the job description I am confident that I would be a perfect fit for this position as my interests and qualifications precisely match your requirements.* *I am applying for the Entry-Level Information Architect position I received via email from the Usability listserv on October 17th. My education and work experience qualifies me for this job.*
Middle paragraph(s) **Deepen Interest — I 激发兴趣** **Create Desire — D 创造需求**	• Why you are qualified for the position • What you have to offer Evidence for skill / experience 1 • *Identify a past or current job, class, or activity* • *Discuss your role, in context to how it exemplifies your skill / experience 1* • *State the accomplishment of your work* Evidence for skill / experience 2/3 • *Identify a different past or current job, class, or activity* • *Discuss your role, in context to how it exemplifies your skill / experience 2 and 3* • *State the accomplishment of your work* Show how your skills match the specific requirements of the job. Explain how these could benefit the company.	*With my background in art and psychology, I am confident that I would make a very successful and creative Studio Assistant. Having worked for the non-profit organization County Arts, I have been exposed to a number of aspects of the art world. My experience as Artist Assistant at the Museum of Art demonstrates my capability of working with others through the creative process of production while meeting the challenges presented to me.* *Also, my education in psychology has allowed me to learn the nuances of people and has provided me with good investigative and analytical skills that will suit your needs for customer assistance. Through my education and past experiences, I have gained excellent people skills and have utilized these skills in various situations. If chosen for this opening I will bring these skills to the workplace every day.*
	• State your personal traits, especially those compatible with the job requirements such as interpersonal skills, efficiency and time-management abilities.	*While working as an intern at the Iowa State University, I dealt daily and successful with administration, faculty, staff, students and the public.*

(Continued)

Parts	Information to include	Examples
Closing paragraph Encourage Action—A 鼓励行动	• How you'll follow-up Restate your interest in the role or restate your skills briefly Request an interview if appropriate Thank the employer	I would appreciate the opportunity to make a substantial contribution by exploring the business of applied art through your design firm. I welcome the opportunity to meet with you to further discuss my candidacy and will call next week to see if we might arrange a time to speak. Thank you for your time and consideration.
Complimentary close	A farewell line Do not use closings like "Yours" "Warmly" or "Cheers", as they appear unprofessional.	Sincerely / Sincerely yours Faithfully / Yours faithfully (if the recipient's name is unknown)
Signature	Writer's full name	*John Smith* John Smith
Enclosure reference	Include the word "Enclosure" or "Enc." Followed by the word "resume"	Enclosure: Resume

2. E-mail cover letter

Parts	Information to include	Examples
From	Your email addresses (Use a professional email address which includes your first and last name or first initial and last name.)	john.smith@uwex.uwc.edu jsmith@uwex.uwc.edu
To	Recipient's email address (Check the job listing or company website to see if the email address is given.)	
Subject line	State your name, the job title, job posting number or a selling point	• Application for Store Manger position — John Smith • Sales Associate Job #1234 — 10 Years' Experience
Greeting	Greet a particular person, if possible.	• Dear Mr. / Ms. Last Name • Dear Hiring Manager

(Continued)

Parts	Information to include	Examples
Message	• Express your interest in the job. • Describe your previous experience that will show the reader that you are qualified for the position. • Mention your resume is attached to the email (if this is the case). • Close with a thank-you and express your readiness to meet the hiring manager in person for an interview.	I am a senior English major at university of Wisconsin with administrative and publications experience interested in the children's trade division editorial assistant position (#498) advertised on bookjobs.com. The attached cover letter and resume provide details about my background and strong interest in Cricket Hill Press. Please let me know if you have difficulty opening the attachments. I look forward to discussing the position with you.
Closing	For hard-copy cover letter, include your printed full name and handwritten signatures. For email cover letter, include your full name and contact information (email address, your phone number, or full address) employment information (your current job title, and the company you work for).	Sincerely / Best regards John Smith University of Wisconsin john.smith@uwex.uwc.edu 732-757-6329
Attachment	Include the word "Attachment".	Attachment: Resume (used for email cover letter)

Cover letter layout and format

Item	Tips
Length	No longer than one page, usually 3 paragraphs. For email cover letter, the message should be no longer than about one screen.
Font	Professional font (Times New Roman, Palatino, Helvetica, or Arial, Veranda, Calibri) in a 10 to 12 point size. Use the same font and size as you use in your CV if providing a printed copy.
Spacing	Single-space text, double-space between paragraphs. Leave a space between your heading (contact information) and greeting (e.g. "Dear Mr. Roberts"). Leave three spaces between your closing (e.g."Sincerely") and typed name. Margins should be 1 inch on all sides.

(Continued)

Item	Tips
Indention	Either align all paragraphs to the left of the page, or indent the first line of each paragraph to the right depending on the format chosen.
Paper	Print your letter on good quality paper. Acceptable colors are white, pale, or ivory. Do not staple your hard-copy cover letter to your resume. Just place it on top of the resume as you fold the documents to fit into the envelope.

Cover letter guidelines

You cover letter should be:

Clear
• Present your skills, interests, and intentions clearly. Be direct about what you can offer to the organization and back up your claims with evidence.

Customized
• Customize each cover letter to a specific job posting. Use the Job Description as a Guide for your writing.

Concrete
• Use specific and concrete words, especially for your competence.

Concise and to the point
• Don't be wordy. Use short paragraphs, especially at the beginning and end of the letter so that employers can quickly scan your document.
• Keep in under a page. Write 3 or 4 paragraphs with 3 to 7 sentences in each. Typically, write only 200~400 words.

Correct
• Edit and proofread your cover letter to make sure it is error-free.

Consistent
• Anything you say in your cover letter should match your resume.

Professional
• Follow a traditional business letter format. Avoid colloquialism and unnecessary abbreviations.

Reader-friendly
• Use white space, reasonable margins, and bullet points for readability.

Relevant
• Everything should be relevant to the job and company.

 ## III Cover letter examples

1. A master candidate (Science) writes a solicited cover letter for IT internship.

The following is a full block format cover letter and each paragraph has been indented. The candidate does not repeat what's in his resume. He summarizes his key skills and qualifications and markets himself to the employer. Underline the expressions that address his key skills and qualification.

(Revised version)

信头：和简历信头保持一致，也可用传统的信头格式

开头：吸引读者，推销自己

LIN FENG
, Xueyuan Road, Haidian District, Beijing, 1000
Home: (010)-****-**** | Cell: 186********
E-mail: linfeng9999@163.com

April 26, 2018

Dear Mr. Moyle,

When I discovered the software engineering internship with Intel Corporation on LiknedIn.com, I was excited by the opportunity to contribute to your company and engage in continuous learning by collaborating with a team of industry experts. My academic background in computer science coupled with hands-on experience and communication skills has provided me with a strong foundation to exceed the responsibilities of this position.

- **Academic background.** As a postgraduate majoring in Computer Science at ABC University, I have completed courses in computer science, software development methods, programming languages, network systems, and embedded system design, resulting in a 3.7 Major GPA as well as the first-class scholarship for three consecutive years.

- **Hands-on experience.** For the past four years, I have gained valuable experience in coding and software development through academic projects and internships. These experiences have allowed me to hone my skills with tools such as Java, C, C++, SQL, and Visual Basic, and to develop my ability to troubleshoot and solve problems in a timely and accurate manner. My recent internship experience at ABC Company has demonstrated my ability to quickly learn new tools when necessary.

- **Communication skills.** Through my project and internship experience, I have developed the initiative and communication abilities to be an effective communicator and leader within a team. I am well prepared to collaborate with interdisciplinary engineering teams.

I believe my solid knowledge of computer science coupled with my practical programming experience will be an asset to this position. I look forward to meeting with you to further discuss my suitability for this position. I can be contacted at 186-123-4567. Thank you for your time and consideration.

Sincerely,

Lin Feng
Lin Feng

Uses the exactly same header and front as his resume.

Expresses enthusiasm about joining the organization
Outlines his qualifications.

Includes a handwritten signature in a hard-copy letter.

Mentions specific position and how you learned about it.

2. A fresh graduate (Political Science) writes an email cover letter to apply for the post of office manager.

The following is a 4-paragraph formal email cover letter. Unlike the brief email cover letter of the same candidate (see Section 1, Task 5), this letter markets her skills needed for the job and details her relevant experience in office administration though her concentration is in political science. This letter uses full-block format and all items are flush with the left margin. Underline the statements that demonstrate what she can offer to the employer or serve as a link to the company's needs or job requirements.

Note: If the candidate is not sure whether the employer would prefer to read a cover letter in the body of email or to read attachments, she can send them both ways in a single message.

From: Sarah Jones sarahjones@yahoo.com   Sent: June 5, 2016
To: corefact-career@gamail.com
Subject: Office Manager Position Application- Sarah Jones
Attachments: SarahJones CoverLetter.pdf
             SarahJones Resume.pdf

> *The subject line indicates the position sought and the name of the candidate.*

Dear Ms. Castro,

　　I am interested in applying for the Office Manager position you have recently posted on dayjob.com. I believe my substantial experience in office management combined with my superb interpersonal and communication skills will be of particular benefit to your organization.

> *Mentions specific position and how you learned about it.*

　　As indicated in my attached resume, I have had the firsthand exposure to office management thanks to my internships at Agway and Nelmar Construction. My prior positions have enabled me to develop diverse administrative skills including daily office operations, executive support, and human resources. My strong organizational skill can be evidenced by the successful implementation of a new efficiency-enhancing workflow at Agway, which streamlined our office procedures, resulting in 20% increase in office efficiency. I believe that it will be equally successful when applied to your business.

> *Highlights the relevant work experience*
>
> *Includes specific accomplishments pertinent to the job description.*

　　I also possess excellent interpersonal and communication skills that your company requires. My internships and campus activities have taught me to communicate effectively with everyone in a manner that would develop relationships and trust. In addition, I am an adept writer / proofreader and enjoy using my strong writing abilities to create different documents from emails to financial statement.

> *Emphasizes the target skills.*

　　I am confident that I would be able to create a smooth-running office with my skills and dedication. I welcome the opportunity to talk with you about my qualifications. Thank you for your time and consideration. I look forward to hearing from you.

　　Sincerely,
　　Sarah Jones

> *Demonstrates confidence and value to the company. Indicates the desire for a personal interview.*

开头：直接点出自己的专长

中间：突出成就和能力，说明为何符合工作要求，激发读者兴趣；略去不相关的教育背景

结尾：表达自信和希望面试的愿望

3. A sophomore (Law) writes an unsolicited application letter seeking a law job.

The candidate inquires about the possible unadvertised job openings by referencing a mutual acquaintance. The letter is in full block format.

Morris Green
248 School Road, Winnipeg,
MB R3Y 8T6
(204) 568-9856
mgreen@cc.umanitoba.ca

May 20, 2016

Mr. George Jacobs
Director of Human Resources
Communication Canada Inc.
1300 River St. W.
Winnipeg, Manitoba
R7B 4H2

Re: Application for Summer Associate Position

Dear Mr. Jacobs,

    I am a second-year law student at the University of Manitoba, and I am writing regarding the possible position of Summer Associate. I would be available to work for any or all of the period between June 15 and August 20, 2016.

    As a Manitoba native, I was familiar with your firm long before I entered law school. I also had the pleasure of hearing your partner, Joe Blue, speak at a recent law school symposium regarding the firm's labor and employment law practice. The firm's representation of management in the recent mining company litigation was quite impressive. *[Inquires about possible openings. No specific position or reference where he saw the job ad.]*

    I have been interested in labor and employment matters since college. My undergraduate training in management sciences helped me develop an understanding of the fundamentals of employment relationships. During the past semester, I completed an externship with a corporation that had a unionized workforce, so I was able to gain experience firsthand in that unique working environment. In addition, I wrote a research paper about the employment relationship termination legislation, and I have enclosed a copy of that paper as a writing sample. *[Demonstrates familiarity with the employer and mentions the partner's name to engage the reader. Relates the undergraduate training, externship, and a research paper to the employer's business.]*

    I would appreciate the opportunity to meet with you in person and to discuss any job openings within your organization. I prefer to handle employment litigation matters but am willing to deal with other legal issues as well. Please call me at 215-890-3465 or contact me by email at mgreen@cc.umanitoba.ca. Thank you for considering my application. *[Requests an interview and expresses interest in the job.]*

    Sincerely,

Morris Green
Morris Green

Enclosures

4. A master candidate (Engineering) writes a solicited application letter for the R & D position.

Anna Gear
annagearannagear@andrew.cmu.edu
(412)-555-123

September 30, 2018

Awesome Engineering Co,
5678 Main Street Pittsburgh, PA 15213

Dear Recruiting Manager,

  I am writing to apply for the R & D Engineer position, which was shared with me by Bob Smith at the Technical Opportunities Conference 2018 at Carnegie Mellon University (CMU). Currently, I am pursuing a Master's degree in Mechanical Engineering at CMU with an expected completion date of May 2019. I believe that my professional experience in the field of Mechanical Engineering, specifically in mechanical product design and development, coupled with the research I am currently conducting at CMU have provided me with the product design, collaboration and project management skills needed to solve advanced engineering problems and be successful in this role.

  Prior to CMU, I spent two years working on product research and development at National Engineering, Inc., where I contributed to the area of advanced product technology development and collaborated with a team of experts in the field of Mechanical Engineering. As part of the research team, I designed and developed two new one way clutch technologies for the two wheeler industry. I also served as the lead engineer in the design and development of a new seal mechanism which provides zero grease leakage and a longer running life. In additional to leadership roles, I collaborated with NEI's product design team on two projects, improving thrust load carrying capacity for a ball bearing and large radial-axial load carrying bearing design, which have been submitted for patents at the Indian Patent Office. This practical experience in mechanical engineering design and development, as well as working with a collaborative team, has given me the skillset to excel in this role.

  My past professional experience and master's research project are similar to the position you are offering: each involves finding the root cause of a problem, mapping a plan to tackle the problem and designing the mechanisms that can solve it in a cost effective and efficient manner. My master's research project at CMU is directed towards the design and development of Fall Aid Health Care devices, where I am leading the project and product design process to create a novel device and solve a real world problem. I have a proven track record in the field of product design and development and I believe I can make a positive impact in solving complex engineering problems as well as driving innovative results.

  I have always enjoyed research and creative problem solving and I believe that my experience will be of value in this role. If given the opportunity, I know I will be a strong asset to your company. Thank you for your time and consideration and I hope to hear from you soon.

  Best Regards,
  Anna Gear

(Source: https://www.cmu.edu/career/documents/sample-resumes-cover-letters/Cover_Letter_Guide_2018.pdf)

IV Writing skills

Selling Yourself in a Cover Letter

A cover letter is a sales letter that sells you as a candidate. Its purpose is to make a quick positive impression on your potential employer and get you an interview. When you market yourself to the prospective employer, you should think carefully what the employer needs and what you can offer, try to impress the employer with attention-getting opening and closing lines and demonstrate your match for the job throughout your letter.

One of the common mistakes many job candidates make is using a generic template to build their cover letters and sending the same cover letter to every employer. It's critical to personalize your cover letter and tailor your cover letter to a specific posting. This not only shows the employer your strong interest in the position and the company, but also allows you to personalize the cover letter so that you can set yourself apart from other candidates.

Writing an attention-getting opening paragraph

Many cover letters start with a generic opening line, which merely identifies the position you are applying for and how you learned of this position. To get noticed immediately, your letter must state some eye-catching things about yourself in relation to the job that will cause the reader to want to continue. You can start your cover letter in one of the following ways:

- **Start with company facts** or the things you like about the company.
- **Highlight your impressive skills or accomplishments** that fit the company's needs.
- **Convey enthusiasm or passion** for the job / company.
- **Mention a personal referral** who refers you to the position.
- **Use keywords** from the job posting.

Conclude (the paragraph) with a "bridge" or an "umbrella" sentence that includes the qualifications you plan to discuss in the body paragraphs.

Task 6. Review the following statements. Decide which statement can grab the reader's attention and which technique is used for opening the cover letter. Complete the table below by putting the number of the statement in the right box.

(1) Candace Peters suggested I apply for this position because she knows: ① My software solutions achieved 97% performance-to-goals at Uber, and ② You're looking for a developer with speed and efficiency, which my resume demonstrates.

(2) I'm interested in the Accountant position and I want to find a place to use the skills I acquired in college as a Business Accounting major. I have a degree from Kean University, and

after I graduated in 2012 I worked for ABC Corporation.

(3) My name is Jane Doe. I graduated from Bates College in 2015 with a degree in marketing, and I'm looking for a job in a relevant field. I have attached my resume for your review. I'm sure that I will be a good fit at your company.

(4) My computer skills developed from childhood, plus my well-honed interest in technology advances, and my recently completed education in computer science make me a strong candidate for a position as an entry-level software engineer at your highly regarded company.

(5) Throughout my studies at Champlain College, my professors have often mentioned ABC Software Consulting and the many interesting engineering projects your company has been involved with. Your reputation for innovation and integrity is well known. It seems to me that ABC Software Consulting would be the ideal place to learn "best practices" of a game company. In fact, that's why I am writing to you.

(6) While completing my degree in media communications and technology last year, I cultivated a true passion for video work. I'm thrilled to contribute my skills to Southeast NewsVideo. I'm confident I am the passionate and hardworking candidate you've been looking for.

Generic opener		( )
Attention-grabbing opener	Start with company facts or your knowledge of the company.	( )
	Highlight your impressive skills or accomplishments.	( )
	Convey enthusiasm or passion.	( )
	Mention a personal referral.	( )

Writing persuasive middle paragraphs

The middle paragraphs give you an opportunity to convince the employer to accept your application for the desired job. The key to a persuasive cover letter is tailoring details about your experience and skills set and making a connection between your qualifications and the company's job requirements or business needs.

1. Identify your top 2~3 selling points that are relevant to the job requirements.

Based on the research on the company and job posting, pick 2~3 key selling points by asking yourself: *How am I different? How has my unique experience or strength prepared me for this position? What do they need? Why should the employer be interested in me?* A college student's cover letter usually addresses three elements: your academic background, practical experience, and personal qualities.

  e.g. Based on my knowledge of and interest in financial services industry, ability to manage a wide array of tasks, and strong work ethic, I believe I can support you in the Fund Accountant position at your firm.

2. Prioritize your selling points according to the degree of relevance or how well they match the job requirements.

Guide the reader by summarizing your selling point in the opening paragraph and explaining how your selling points match their needs in the middle paragraphs.

3. Promote your selling points and explain how you meet the employers' needs.

Each body paragraph focuses on one selling point or qualification, with details and examples that support this qualification.

Explain how your background and experience qualifies you for this job and what you can offer.

In connecting your qualifications to the job requirements, keep the following points in mind:

(1) <u>Focus on the employer's needs</u> rather than your needs or goals.

Weak: *The reason that I am applying for this position is that I want to train myself before I graduate and I just want to work in the Sales and Marketing Department of an Electronics Company.*

Better: *My proven dedication to optimizing customer service and sales success will contribute immensely to the success of your team in this role.*

(2) <u>Show, don't tell</u>. Provide details and examples to support your claims. Specifics make you look interested, well-informed, and qualified. Emphasize your accomplishments instead of day-to-day responsibilities.

Weak: *I am a self-starter and a quick study.*   *[Vague claim]*

Better: *Working for Corporation × demonstrates that I am a self-starter and a quick learner Only one week after being hired, my supervisor was transferred to another office, and I successfully managed and operated the sales department from that day forward, increasing our sales by 20 percent in just two years.*   *[Specific examples]*

Weak: *I graduated with a Masters in Chemical Engineering from Carnegie Mellon University. This past year, I was a research assistant with Dr. ××× and I worked alongside other chemical engineers to ensure we completed our project by the deadline.*

[List facts or day-to-day responsibilities]

Better: *My research in the Chemical Engineering department at Carnegie Mellon University has been focused on migration of electrolytic components through separator membranes. As a research assistant with Dr. ×××, I worked towards the device implementation of semiconducting conjugated polymers and <u>acquired integrated technical judgment and a background in</u> modeling from first principles. <u>Through my research assistantship I have been prepared to provide materials expertise to your company</u>.*

[Emphasize results and suitability]

(3) <u>Use the keywords in job postings</u> to bring attention to your match for the position.

e.g. Your need for a <u>top-performing, results-proven outside sales professional</u> caught my attention. As an award-winning <u>B2B sales specialist</u>, I would be a perfect candidate for this post *by offering my five years of outside B2B sales experience.*

☞ Read the sample cover letters in Section Ⅲ. Identify the key selling points of each job candidate and analyze how writers promote their selling points.

Task 7. Read the first draft of your cover letter and rethink your key selling points that will add value to the employer.

Ask yourself: *What is the one thing that makes you unique? What makes you better than other candidates applying for a similar position with this company? What can you offer that no other applicant can? What is the one reason the employer should want to hire you above all other candidates?* Also, look at the job posting, which will tell you the skills required.

Identify 2~3 key qualifications for the job and state them in the first paragraph. Put your most relevant match in the second paragraph, the next relevant in the third and so on.

Opening paragraph: Summary of my key selling points / qualifications _____

Middles paragraphs:
Key selling point 1: _____ + Proof / Detail / accomplishments : _____
Key selling point 2: _____ + Proof / Detail / accomplishments : _____
Key selling point 3: _____ + Proof / Detail / accomplishments : _____

Task 8. Match the expressions in the left column that describe the job candidate's skill and experience to the expressions in the right column that connect the qualifications to the employer's needs.

Qualifications	Connection to the job requirements
(1) Working as an office manager and receptionist for a pediatric practice, I learned the importance of meticulous recordkeeping.	(a) The experience that I believe would transfer well to the position of paralegal.
(2) As a graduate student in MIT's Technology and Policy Program, I spend every day at the cutting edge of the energy sector. Graduate classes in energy economics, energy ventures and strategy, and technology policy.	(b) Your school emphasizes its unique position as a school that caters to both inner-city and suburban students, so I think my varied experiences would make me an asset to your program.
(3) I have been consistently engaged in conducting long-term and short-term research projects, most of which involved meticulous investigation and qualitative research.	(c) This skill should prove particularly useful when reviewing health care litigation documents.
(4) I have experience teaching elementary-level students in a variety of settings. I am currently teaching third-grade children at an inner-city school. As a former education coordinator at a local museum, I also have experience teaching fourth-grade students in a small suburban school system.	(d) Have prepared me well to make a significant contribution to your organization and offer the expert services that set it apart from competitors.

Writing a strong closing paragraph

The closing paragraph usually thanks the reader for taking his or her time to consider your cover letter and resume and to suggest an interview. The closing paragraph is also a good place to impress the employer with your unique qualification and the value you bring to the company.

Task 9. Compare different ways of ending a cover letter and comment on the underlined expressions.

Generic closing line	Strong closing line
• Thank you for reviewing my credentials. I look forward to learning more about the opportunity. • Enclosed is my resume for your review. I look forward to discussing my experience and this opportunity with you in person. Please contact me by phone or email if you have any further questions. Thank you for your time and consideration.	(1) I would welcome the chance to discuss your digital marketing objectives and show you how my success at ABC can translate into digital and online marketing growth for XYZ. (2) Based on my knowledge and experience, I am committed for the best performance to your company. I am confident that I will definitely add great value to the department of communication and create flawless communication system in the company. (3) I am very excited to learn more about this opportunity and share how I will be a great fit for XYZ Corporation. (4) If you need someone who is highly motivated, eager to learn, and willing to work hard to succeed, please contact me at phone.

Getting your cover letter's tone right

As a general rule, your cover letter should be formal, confident, courteous, and positive. Your upbeat and enthusiastic tone and positive language will likely get a response from the hiring manager. When introducing yourself to the potential employer, avoid bragging, exaggerating or sounding too casual, impolite, arrogant or humble.

Task 10. Read the following statements and decide if they are written in the right tone for a cover letter. Put a cross (×) after the statement which you think the tone is inappropriate. Then discuss in pairs how to improve the tone.

(1) I am confident that my experience and references will show you that I can fulfill the requirements of your secretarial position.

(2) Hello. I am just wondering if you are still offering a security guard position.

(3) I am only average at Excel and incapable of HTML.

(4) Could we set up an interview so I can explain in more detail how my qualifications match the needs of Oakland Elementary?

(5) I hope this cover letter convinces you of my qualifications enough so that you know I am

a perfect candidate for this position and you must meet me immediately.

(6) I guess the only reason I'm applying is that I studied International Relations. I know I am not tailor made for the job, but I am smart and easy to train.

(7) Respected leader, Hello! Thank you in advance for taking the time out of your busy schedule to read my cover letter and resume.

V Exercises and Practice

Writing the opening paragraph

Task 11. Write a complete sentence to state your candidacy by using the words provided. Add some words or change the form of the provided words where necessary.

Example: would like, submit my application, design consultant, available, XYZ Company

I would like to submit my application for your design consultant position available at XYZ Company.

(1) write, apply, Senior Marketing Officer, post, CareerTimes.com, September 23 2016

_____

(2) accept, my resume, consideration, sales manager position

_____

(3) express, strong interest, position, Research Fellow in Applied Health Research, advertise, on jobs.ac.uk

_____

(4) write, in response to, advertisement, a Legal Assistant, specialize in Criminal Law, appear in the Seattle Times on June 15

_____

Task 12. Combine the loose ideas into one sentence by using the appropriate structures provided below. Eliminate unnecessary words and subordinate where possible. Avoid monotony in writing or a succession of short and loose sentences.

As a / an..., I...   With / Based on..., I...
My...combined with / coupled with...

> Many short or choppy sentences in succession often repeat the same word and your writing appears unsophisticated.

Examples:

I am a recent graduate. I have writing, editing, and administrative experience.
I believe I am a strong candidate for the position at the 123 Publishing Company.

As a recent graduate with writing, editing, and administrative experience, I believe I am a strong candidate for a position at the 123 Publishing Company.

Unit 2 Cover Letters

I possess strong communication and technology skills and background in marketing.
I could make a strong contribution to the CICA team.
With my strong communication and technology skills and background in marketing. I could make a strong contribution to the CICA team.

I have educational background in public administration and foreign policy. I worked as an intern at the Department of Justice and the Office of International Affairs. These experiences have strengthened my communication and analytical skills, which will provide me with strong foundations to exceed the responsibilities of the ABC Summer Fellowship role.
*My educational background in public administration and foreign policy **coupled with** internship at the Department of Justice and the Office of International Affairs **have strengthened** my communication and analytical skills, **providing** me with strong foundation to exceed the responsibilities of the ABC Summer Fellowship role.*

(1) I am an engineer. I have got a bachelor's degree in both computer science and software engineering.
I am excited to apply for the opening for a software engineer at XYZ.

_____

_____

(2) I have a proven track record in delivering projects ahead of time and under budget. I will make a successful addition to your engineering team.

_____

_____

(3) I receive academic training in strategic analysis. I also demonstrate strong management skills, which can be evidenced by my leadership role at Youthbuild. These qualifications would enable me to expand your company's growth and work towards a more sustainable future.

_____

_____

Writing middle paragraphs

Task 13. Translate the expressions in the brackets into English. Use the expressions in the box below where possible. Please note how the writer describes relevant experience and skills and make a connection between your qualifications and the employer's needs. Underline the expressions which emphasize the relevant skills and accomplishments.

work as / serve as / act as	this experience / position / role	allow / enable / compel me to do sth.	
gain valuable experience	gain insight into provide…with…	interact with take part in	
be aware of the importance of	demonstrate / show / develop / sharpen / improve / strengthen…skills		

(1) _____ (在2012年暑期实习期间) with the U.S.-China Energy Cooperation Program in Beijing, I _____ (担任联络人) among the U.S. agencies and their Chinese counterparts. I _____ (不仅更加了解) Sino-American government relations and large-scale event planning from this experience, _____ (而且提高了……的能力) to multi-task, prioritize my tasks, and to pay close attention to details.

　　(2) This past summer, I _____ (我担任研究项目的主研人) analyzing Medicaid claims data of enrollees diagnosed with Manor Depression. The project was largely quantitative and relied heavily on statistical analyses, _____ (使我熟练掌握) Excel, SPSS, and the art of making data tables and graphs.

　　(3) I am confident _____ (学习期间获取的知识) at Boston University will prove beneficial at YearUp. I have thoroughly enjoyed and succeeded in my Statistics and Econometric Analysis classes. _____ (这些课程让我理解了) statistical programs, such as STATA and Excel, and an even greater interest in financial services. The quantitative focus of my economic major requires acute attention to detail and _____ (锻炼我的分析能力).

　　(4) _____ (课外我积极参与校园活动) as the chair of Student Union and orientation advisor for the past three years. _____ (这些领导职位让我可以和各种不同的人打交道). As an orientation advisor, I continually build relationships with prospective students and their parents _____ (展示出我出色的组织能力和交流能力).

　　(5) My first experience aboard was during high school. I studied in Latin America with a program similar to yours. _____ (这段经历让我意识到跨文化学习和全球思维的重要性).

　　(6) Since earning a bachelor's degree in electrical engineering (BSEE), I have worked for the last 5 years as an electrical engineer for XYZ Corporation. _____ (在这个岗位中，我获得了宝贵的……经验) maintaining, troubleshooting, upgrading and repairing plant electrical equipment. _____ (这段经历给我打下坚实的基础) within the heavy industrial manufacturing sector in addition to proven success in extending the average life of electronic industrial systems and components by up to 25%.

Putting it together

Task 14. Complete the following cover letter by filling in the blanks with the appropriate prepositions.

　　A strong interest _____ Design and Modeling has encouraged me to apply _____ your internship position at MerryMill. As a candidate _____ the Master's degree _____ Mechanical Engineering at Tufts University, I am prepared to contribute the skills I have acquired in my classes and research _____ your world-class work in acoustics.

My thesis _____ analysis of Pinch and Roll process used to manufacture aircraft turbine and compressor blades, and a course project _____ Manufacturing Design and Cost Analysis of Turbine Disk, exposed me _____ manufacturing practices and familiarized me _____ solid modeling software like AutoCAD and Pro Engineer. I am confident that I can manage high level Design and Modeling projects based _____ my understanding and use of FEM packages like Deform and Analysis, CAD tools, and Mathematics based software MathCAD.

The rigor of my courses at Tufts coupled _____ projects and term paper presentations for my Master's program have developed my analytical aptitude and communication skills. In addition, as Vice President of the Indian Society at Tufts, I have organized social and cultural events to promote appreciation of diversity and I have raised funds to provide scholarships _____ Indian students. These experiences demonstrate my organizational and management skills and ability to work well as part of a team.

I would like to discuss your internship opportunity with you _____ your convenience. I can be reached _____ (phone) or (email). Thank you for reviewing my credentials for this position.

Assignments

1. Peer review.

Use the following checklist to critique your own cover letter and two cover letters written by your classmates.

Cover Letter Checklist

Strategy	Be tailored and personalized to an individual employer. • Research the company's needs. • Explain how your skills and background match those needs. • Stress what you can do for the company rather than what the company can do for you.
Content	**Heading** includes your address and contact information, followed by the date, and the employer's name and address. **Salutation** is formal: Using the hiring manager's name if known or a general salutation such as Dear Hiring Manager. Avoid "Dear Sir or Madam," "To whom it may concern". **The subject line** for email message includes the name of the position and your name. **Introduction:** (1) Tells the employer why you are writing the letter and names the position for which you are applying. (2) Shows your interest in the company or makes a strong claim about your candidacy that previews 1~3 qualifications you discuss in the body paragraphs.

(Continued)

Content	**Body paragraphs:** (1) Each paragraph discusses one qualification highlighted in the introduction. (2) Paragraphs focus on connecting your skills, qualifications and education to the company and / or position. (3) Specifics details and / or examples are provided. **Conclusion:** (1) Reminds the reader why you are a strong match for the position or shows your interest and enthusiasm. (2) Includes a call to action — requests an interview, refers to future contact, etc. (3) Mentions the other document(s) you are enclosing or attaching. (4) Provides your contact information (email and phone number). (5) Thanks the reader for his / her time and consideration.
Format & design	• Use the correct business letter format or email cover letter format. • Length of about half a page to one page. • A consistent look between your resume and cover letter. • A balance of the white space used. Not too much, nor too little.
Style & tone	• The paragraphs are coherent and the sentences are concise. • The tone is appropriate — confident, polite, businesslike.
Mechanics	No spelling, punctuation, and grammatical errors.

2. Revise your cover letter.

Revise your letter based on class discussion, peer critiques, and the instructor's comments. Turn in the final version of your cover letter and resume on good quality paper along with your job advertisement.

3. Review samples.

Find and review cover letter samples from professionals in your industry. Learn the writing techniques and useful expressions. Make sure you don't simply copy someone else's work.

Unit 3　Job Interviews

> Job interviews are a critical part of landing a job. In interviews, if you can convince a recruiter that you fit the organization's culture and job description, you will get much closer to an offer. This unit helps you prepare for job interviews and impress potential employers. You will learn about different types of interviews, common interview questions and answers, typical questions that can be asked during a job interview. You will also learn the basic steps and techniques for having a successful interview.

Objectives

After completing this unit, you will be able to

◆ Conduct basic interview research to prepare for a successful job interview;
◆ Identify different types of job interviews and common interview questions;
◆ Deal effectively with interview questions using the right strategies;
◆ Develop a powerful elevator pitch for your interview;
◆ Structure a response using the Situation-Task-Action-Result model.

I　Pre-class activities

✎Research and Explore

Task 1. Do preliminary reading and research on the following questions and get prepared for class discussion.

(1) What are the ways of creating a positive first impression in job interview?

_____

_____

(2) What are common interview questions? What are some difficult interview questions?

Task 2. Prepare for your job interview.

(1) **Interview** some final year undergraduate or graduate students in your school to talk about their interview experience. Record the kind of questions they were asked and their advice about how to prepare for job interviews.

(2) **Review your research on the company and the position.**

Think about how to demonstrate your knowledge of the company in your responses to the questions. Determine your skills, strengths and accomplishments that align with job requirements. Think of situations where you have demonstrated that you meet the requirements. Prepare "stories" you can share briefly in the interview.

(3) **Do some research on your interviewer.**

Look for publicly available information on your interviewer from their LinkedIn Profiles or company website (What are their names? What do they do?). Try to identify something that you both have in common (hometown, college degree, school, hobby, etc.).

(4) **Prepare a list of possible interview questions and write down your answer to each question.**

(5) **Prepare several questions ready to ask the interviewer** such as the questions about the company and position.

(6) **Prepare how to deal with negative aspects of your background,** i.e., low grade point average, no participation in outside activities, no related work experience.

(7) **Research career fields and salary averages and what your skills and level of experience are worth.** Develop a salary range and a proper response to the question about your salary requirements.

Case study

Task 3. Lin Feng will be interviewed for the software engineering intern position in Intel. Before the interview, he prepares a one-minute self-introduction. However, after consulting with a Career Counselor and some experienced job seekers, he decides to revise his self-introduction. Work in pairs or groups and identify the problems with this script.

> Hello, interviewers. I'm so honored to have this opportunity to introduce myself. My name is Lin Feng. My hometown is Chengdu, a beautiful city in Sichuan Province. I am a postgraduate student from ABC University and I major in Computer Science. I'm here to apply for the intern position of software engineer. While in college, I spend most of my time on study. I not only have acquired basic knowledge of my major but also participated in many projects, sharpening my programming skills. Besides, I have passed CET-4 and CET-6. I have team spirit and good communication skills. I hope I can work in your company so that I can use my knowledge and skills.

☞ See the revised version of this self-introduction in Section Ⅲ.

Task 4. Sarah Jones is now informed of an incoming interview for the office manager position in XYZ Company. She reviews the job description and her resume again and notes down two points that the interviewers may think make her under-qualified for the position:

• Major is not closely relevant to the job;
• Internships at small companies and lack of experience as an office manager.

Discuss in groups how to explain your qualifications to the interviewer if you were Sarah Jones. Anticipate other difficult questions she might encounter in job interview.

☞ See Sarah's responses to interview questions in Section Ⅲ.

Ⅱ Introduction

Job interview is one of the most important parts of job search. This is your opportunity to shine and show the value you will bring to the organization and land the job. To leave a positive impression on your interviewer, you should be able to present yourself professionally, communicate effectively with the interviewer, appropriately respond to interview questions in a stressful situation, and demonstrate appropriate manners.

The key to a successful interview is being prepared. You should know what you need to do before, during and after the interview to ensure your success. Here are the steps you can take to prepare:

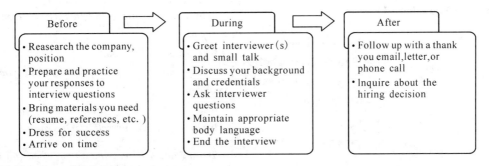

Types of job interviews

You may run into different situations in job interviews. Find out what type of interview you will have. Here are common types of interviews:

• **One-on-one interview:** Just you and one interviewer, the most common type of interview.

• **Panel interview:** You are interviewed by a group of interviewers taking turns to ask you their questions.

• **Telephone or screening interview:** Phone interviews are often conducted as a first-round screening before inviting you to an on-site interview.

• **Video interview:** A "person-to-person" interview by video using Skype, Google Chat or smartphones.

• **Group interview:** Multiple candidates are interviewed by a panel or one interviewer at the same time. It's a way to make the hiring process more efficient and to see how job seekers react in a stressful or group situation.

• **Stress Interview:** Questions intended to make you uncomfortable and a test how you will handle stress on the job.

• **Luncheon Interview:** Interview conducted in a restaurant to assess how well you handle yourself in social situations.

Types of interview questions

Depending on the position you apply for, you may be asked questions from any of following different categories during the course of your interview:

Type of question	Purpose	Examples
Traditional questions / Common questions	**Verification questions** Objectively verify your background, credentials, experience and understand more about your experience, background, and personal qualities.	• Tell me about yourself. • What was your GPA? • What did you learn in that class? • How long were you at _____? • What were your responsibilities in that position?
	Opinion questions Subjectively analyze how you would respond in a series of scenarios.	• Why are you interested in this position/our company? • Why should we hire you? • Tell me about an accomplishment that you are proud of. • What are your greatest strengths and weaknesses? • Where do you see yourself in 5/10 years?
Behavioral questions	Learn about your past behaviors in specific work situations and predict future performance. Use STAR Method to answer the questions.	• Tell me about / Describe a time when you were able to successfully convince someone to see things your way. • Give an example of a time you were given no direction, but took the initiative to get something done. • Describe a situation in which you used persuasion to successfully convince someone to see things your way.

(Continued)

Type of question	Purpose	Examples
Brainteaser questions	Test intelligence; evaluate mental your creative ability.	• What is 1 000 divided by 73? • How many ping pong balls could fit in a Volkswagen?
Case / Technical questions	Evaluate your discipline-specific knowledge, problem-solving abilities through potential case situations.	• What development tools have you used? • Your client is a $300 million a year copper mining company. This year it has lost $50 million. How do you turn it around?
Dumb questions	Find out if you are capable of an original thought. There is not necessarily a right or wrong answer.	• What kind of animal would you like to be? • What color best describes you?

Common interview questions and answers

Questions & Tips for answering	Examples
Tell me about yourself.	
<u>The interviewer wants to:</u> find out what are your selling points for this job, whether you've done research about the company and why you are interested in this position right now. <u>You should:</u> • know their needs • give a quick overall summary of you • focus on the part of you which makes you the best candidate for the position • keep your answer brief and relevant <u>You shouldn't:</u> • just repeat what's on your resume • talk about your personal life outside your work • just tell instead of selling yourself	*(Good)* "I am energetic and a good communicator. Working in sales for two years helped me build confidence, and taught me the importance of customer loyalty. I've also got a track record of success. In my last role, I launched a company newsletter, which helped me build on our existing relationships and create new ones. Because of this, we ended up seeing a revenue increase of 10% over two years. I'm also really interested in how companies can use web tools to better market themselves, would be committed to building on your existing platform." *(Bad)* "Well, I graduated four years ago from University of Michigan with a Bachelor's in biology. But I decided that wasn't the right path for me, so I switched gears and got my first job, working in sales for a startup. Then I went on to work in a law firm. After that I took a few months off to travel. Finally, I came back and worked in marketing again. Now I'm here, looking for a more challenging marketing role."

(Continued)

Questions & Tips for answering	Examples
What is your greatest strength?	
<u>The interviewer wants to:</u> • know how well you know your strengths and whether your strengths align with the needs of the company and the job responsibilities. <u>You should:</u> • discuss those strengths that are important for the position or set your apart from other candidates **(Strength)** • support your statements with examples of experiences in which you have demonstrated your strengths **(Proof)** Types of strengths: **Job-specific** (computer skills, technical training, product or industry knowledge) **Transferrable** (organizational and planning skills / perseverance / communication skills / leadership ability / problem solving/creativity) **Personal characteristics** (punctual, self-motivated, reliable, adaptable, stress tolerance, flexibility / independence etc.) <u>You shouldn't:</u> • give empty clichés without the back of examples • choose irrelevant strengths	*(Good)* "One of my greatest strengths is my proficiency in C++. I have a tremendous amount of experience working with the language." *(job-specific)* "I pride myself on my leadership skills. [Strength] I've been an IT project manager for 5 years, managing 10 major projects. All of those projects completed on schedule, met their specifications, and were considered successes. In addition, I was able to train 4 team members so they were promoted to project management positions." [Proof] *(transferrable)* "I am an eager learner. [Strength] As you can see from my resume, I've taken advantage of every opportunity to develop technical knowledge in this field such as participating in the projects, taking part in competitions. Plus, I also attended many forums to update my understanding of the what is new out there."[Proof] *(characteristics)* *(Bad)* "I'm people's person and very hard-working." *(cliché)*
What is your greatest weakness?	
<u>The interviewer wants to:</u> • know what risks they are taking by hiring you • assess your self-awareness and insight • see how you react to stress questions <u>You should:</u> (1) Acknowledge one or two minor weaknesses. (2) Explain how you are fixing or you have overcome.	*(Good)* "I'm impatient with people who don't work at the same pace as me but I'm learning to manage this. I make sure that they have the right resources for the job, I follow up to see that they are on track and I step in and help when needed." "Because I concentrate so much on what I'm doing, I often have a hard time juggling interruptions and other things that come up."

(Continued)

Questions & Tips for answering	Examples

Types of weakness:
• The weakness is unrelated to the position
  fear of speaking before groups, or lack of computer skills (if the job doesn't require it)
• The weakness is a strength in disguise
  lack of attention to detail, as a result of seeing too much of the big picture; difficulty multitasking, due to an intense focus on the task at hand
• The weakness that you're working to improve
 	
You shouldn't:
• give a huge weakness that cannot be corrected or will have a negative impact on your job performance
• give cliché answers
	"My presentational skills are quite weak. But I have been on several presentational seminars and I've joined a speech club, and I found that really helped my confidence."
	
	(Bad) "I have a tendency to make a lot spelling mistakes I think that's why I got fired from my last job." *(Secretary)*
	"I'm too polite" "I'm a perfectionist". *(Cliché)*
	"I can't think of any relevant weaknesses."

Where do you see yourself in 5 years' time? / What are your goals for the next couple of years?	
The interviewer wants to: • look for people who have directions and some plan for their future • know how committed you are to the career and the company, and what is your motivation in applying for this position **You should:** • relate your personal career goal to the job, the company, and the industry • explain you want to grow and excel within their company • focus on the near term and keep it reasonable **You shouldn't:** • set out very specific, rigid goals • have no career plan	*(Good)* "In the near term, I would like to develop myself to become the best _____ possible, learning as much as I can about the role and about how I can best serve the needs of the department and the company. In the longer-term, I would like to grow with a company where I can continue to learn, take on additional responsibilities, and contribute as much value as I can. I love that your company emphasizes professional development opportunities. I intend to take advantage of all of these." "I want to have developed new skills and abilities and to have made the most of my opportunities. This position will give me the opportunity to learn more about managing a work team, and this is a goal of mine. I would like to be recognized as an individual who has really added value to the team and the company." *(Bad)* "I want to be the Vice President within 2 years so I can have my own team." "I'm spontaneous and never plan too far into the future."
Why should we hire you? / Why are you the best candidate for the job?	

(Continued)

Questions & Tips for answering	Examples
The interviewer wants to: give you the open opportunity to sell yourself so that you convince him / her you are the best person for the position **You should:** • match your qualifications to the job requirements • focus on the part of your education, work experience, skills, and accomplishments which make you stand out among all the candidates • highlight the specific benefits you can bring to the company • support your claims with memorable descriptions and / or examples • be straightforward and confident about your abilities • be enthusiastic about why you want this job **You shouldn't:** • tell them what you want out of this job • say that you are the best qualified candidate, without proof or any explanation of your suitability	**(Good)** "Well, I have all of the skills and experience that you're looking for and I'm confident that I would excel in this project management role. It's not just my background leading successful projects for top companies — or my people skills, which have helped me develop great relationships with developers, vendors, and senior managers alike. But I'm also passionate about this industry and I'm driven to deliver high-quality work." "Because I'm the best person for the job. I know you are interviewing other students with similar qualifications. Yet I was awarded the Employee of the Month award as an intern this past summer and was the first intern ever to receive that award. I was given that award over all other nominations of their full-time staff. That award was given due to my delivery on a project that no one else had been able to successfully complete. I not only delivered the project, but I did it while also working on two other projects, both of which were completed during job one summer as an intern. Let me tell you about the project where I won the award…" **(Bad)** "I really need this job and it would be awesome to work here! I think I'm the best candidate for the role."
Why do you want to work for this company? / Why do you choose our company?	
The interviewer wants to: look for people who will mesh with the company **You should:** • include your company research in your answer • find something specific about the company to hook into such as company's products, reputation, mission, vision and successes. How do you complement and contribute to these? **You shouldn't:** • flatter the company excessively • focus on your concerns or benefits • be negative	**(Good)** "I understand this company is expanding, and your website indicates that you are about to launch a number of new products. I would like to be a part of this exciting growth." "This firm is one of the leading accounting firms in this state, with very high customer satisfaction rates. You, advocate strong security measures to protect financial transactions and information. With my background in cyber security, I'm very interested in applying the newest technology plus common sense practices to keep this sensitive information as safe as possible." **(Bad)** "Because your company is in my job search list. My career advisor said you were a good company." "Because I have been rejected from 3 other companies before yours."

(Continued)

Questions & Tips for answering	Examples
Why do you want this job?	
Interviewer wants to: • assess how much you know about the job itself • know whether you are a good fit for them **You should:** show your enthusiasm for the job, how your skills match the role and how you fit into the culture **You shouldn't:** mention salary, hours, or fringe benefits as the primary reasons you want the job. Those reasons will not impress an employer with your fit for their job	*(Good)* "I want the challenge of selling a new product. I consider strategy development one of my key skills and I would like to be able to use it to the fullest in developing strategies for selling this product…" "I am looking for a company where I not only enjoy what I am doing but I can also grow into new positions. In the computer field there are always new tools and technologies coming out. I want a company that allows me to learn more and expand my capabilities into new areas. The fact that you sponsor a week of training every year and that most of the people I've met have been here more than five years shows me that we share the same values."
What kind of salary are you expecting?	
The interviewer wants to: test your money / salary expectations up against the range for the role. If you are outside the allowable range, it may not be worth pursuing you as a candidate **You should:** • give a broad but realistic range for the role • wait until the interviewer introduces the topic of salary • ask about the salary either at the end of the job interview or when you have been offered the job **You shouldn't:** • demand / ask for too much money	*(Good)* "I'm more interested in the role itself than the pay. I'd expect to be paid appropriate range for this role, based on my five years of experience." "I'm looking for a starting salary somewhere between $25 000 and $30 000." *(Bad)* "I'm not sure. How much are you on?" "In my last job I earned 12 000 yuan a month – and now I'm looking for 18 000."

Types of questions a job candidate can ask

Near the end of the interview, you may be asked to ask the interviewers some questions. It's important to have a few questions ready in your mind. By asking intelligent, well-thought-out questions, you show the employer you are serious about the organization and need more information. Questions about salary and benefits are best left until an offer has been extended. Don't ask something you could have found the answers on the company's website.

Be aware of cultural differences when it comes to asking interviewers questions. In many western countries, you are expected to ask the interviewer direct questions during the interview. It shows your initiative, confidence and curiosity. However, in Asian countries your role in the interview may be more passive. If invited to ask questions, your questions may be expected to more general, open-ended, and exploratory in nature rather than detailed and direct. It may not be appropriate to ask targeted questions about payment, working conditions, and job responsibilities, unless specifically invited to do so. Therefore, you should research the specific conventions of individual companies in advance.

Questions to ask	Examples
The company and its leader Executives think big. You should also think big. Asking questions that show you've done your homework or show your interviewer that you can think big-picture, you are interested in the company, and you're wanting to stay with the company long-term.	• Where does \<company\> see itself heading in the next five to ten years? How would the person in this role contribute to this vision? • What are some of the problems your company faces right now? And what is your department doing to solve them? • I read...about your CEO in Business Insider. Can you tell me more about this?
The position Take this opportunity to learn more about the job responsibilities and expectations. Figure out if you can easily see yourself enjoying this role for the foreseeable future. This shows your eagerness about the position.	• Would you describe the duties of the position for me, please? • What are the main challenges or opportunities associated with this position? • What skills do you see as most important in order to be successful in this position? • Beyond the hard skills required to successfully perform this job, what soft skills would serve the company and position best?
Career path and growth Ask employers such questions to show that you care about your future at the company.	• What is the promotion path for this role? • What qualities are the most important for doing well and advancing at the firm? • Where does this role fit in the growth strategy of the company? • Are there training programs available to me so that I can learn and grow professionally?

(Continued)

Questions to ask	Examples
The manager / supervisor Whether you're in the initial discussion with a recruiter or interviewing directly with your potential supervisor, you can find out more about the person you'll be reporting. Decide if you're compatible with their style and preferences.	• *I'd like to know your leadership style. Do you mind describing it to me?* • *Could you tell me what your ideal employee looks like?* • *Can you give me an example of how I would collaborate with my manager?*
The interviewer Questions can help make a better impression on your interviewer.	• *Can you tell me a little about your own experience with the company? What do you enjoy most about working here?* • *Can you walk me through your typical work day?*
The application processes This one tells them you're interested in the role and eager to hear their decision. It shows enthusiasm and eagerness.	• *When do you expect to make a hiring decision for this position?* • *What's your timeline for next steps?* • *Is there anything else I can provide to help you make your decision?*

III Sample interview questions and answers

Lin Feng is interviewed for the software engineer position

Question: Tell me about yourself.

Answer: Hi, my name is Lin Feng and I am currently studying for a master's degree in Computer Science at ABC University. I have a strong interest in programming and hands-on experience using Java, C, and C++ languages to create and implement software applications. I did a couple of internships and projects applying my new coding skills to solve real-world problems. As I often work with teams of peers or IT professionals, I also see myself as a people-oriented person who always performs well in various group projects. My past experiences have shown that I enjoy engaging in projects that require me to work outside my comfort zone and knowledge set, as I continue to learn new languages and development techniques. That's also the reason why I would like to be part of your company where I can further develop myself in IT field and to use my capabilities to serve both your company and your clients.

Question: Why are you interested in our company?

Answer: Well, the Intel reputation is certainly a factor. Your company is known for making a commitment to bettering the community through IT technology in areas like education and environment. I would love the opportunity to join your programs such as Intel Walk Into Community program and University Research Collaboration Program to change the lives of Chinese people. At the same time, I have friends in the industry who have told me about your company's respect for employees and how you create a great environment for rewarding innovation. I think my proactive style would fit in really well here.

(Continued)

Question: Tell us about your most successful project.

Answer: One of the most successful projects I had worked on was a Mobile App for Android called Edu-Life Studio. In 2017, I led a 4-person team to take part in Innovation and Entrepreneurship Competition of ABC University. As the project leader, I built a team and inspired and motivated my team. As the lead developer, I was responsible for the underlying architecture for this App and implementing software solutions. Despite the initial failure, we managed to create a high-quality mobile App using C++ in the fastest possible time. This education and entertainment Mobile App tuned out to be very popular with college students. It had achieved up to 10K downloads with 4+ average rating. This experience has not only sharpened my expertise but also improved my communication and project management skills.

Question: Describe your strengths and weaknesses as a software developer.

Answer: I'm an inquisitive fast learner. I'm eager to learn new languages and look for new solutions. I can quickly research, understand and use unfamiliar software technologies, tools and languages. This is very important in the world of IT. I also have strong communication skills, which I believe is crucial for agile development. Pure coding is not enough for being a great software developer. I can figure things out based on communication with both technical and non-technical people. I am good at managing other people and leading a team.

On the other hand, I am sometimes too result-driven and impatient when I'm working on a project. I never miss a deadline, so I can find myself rushed when I'm working. However, I am aware of this weakness and always remind it to myself to stay patient in job. I've learned to slow down, be more patient, and give each project the careful attention it deserves.

Where do you see yourself in five years?

Answer: As I am more interested in gaining a few years of actual real-world experience, I'd like to work as a full-time staff member of an IT company to expand my skillset in a software engineer role and learn more about the industry. Eventually, I'd like to move into an executive role. Your organization seems to offer employees room to grow internally, which is something that I really value.

Do you have any questions?

Answer: Yes. Could you describe the tasks and assignments I will be involved in if I am offered the position?

Sarah Jones is interviewed for the position of Office Manager

Question: Tell me about yourself.

Answer: I'm Sarah Jones, a recent graduate from California State University. I've always felt that my personality is more suited to office management and I did some intern jobs related to it. I have the experience and the attitude to excel in this office manager position. I have almost two years of administrative and management experience — including two summers interning at Agway and Nelmar, where I was exposed to all aspects of office duties and complete all the office duties to the highest standard. I've also got a track record of success. In my last role, I introduced and implemented a new efficiency-enhancing workflow at Agway, which helped us streamlined our office procedures and achieved 20% increase in office efficiency. Because of this, they invited me back for a second summer job and gave me more responsibilities. I am currently looking for a position that offers both a great challenge and opportunity to leverage my acquired skills. This is why I responded to your advert for this position, and I am hoping you will agree that I am the best fit for this role.

(Continued)

Question: You majored in Political Science. How did that prepare you for an office manager job?

Answer: Although Political Science seems unrelated to this career, I can apply knowledge of political science as I organize activities and structure leadership programs. I know how to develop effective strategies to influence others, gain support from my team, and mediate disputes between team members. As a political science major, I also develop strong writing and communications skills needed for this position. Since I became more interested in administrative jobs, on top of my major courses I took additional courses in business management, accounting, human resources office management, and business law. I believe I am well prepared for this career.

Question: From your resume, I notice that you interned at a small company. Did you pursue a full-time job offer with them? Do you think it is one of your disadvantages?

Answer: Actually, I did very well at my internship, and I had originally assumed that I would stay there once I graduated from college. However, due to economic downturn, they will not be hiring any of the interns they had last summer.

Besides, I don't think interning at small companies is my weakness. I can see that your company currently has over 70 employees. The companies I interned for only had fifteen to twenty employees. I would say my greatest weakness pertaining to this job would be my lack of experience in working for a larger company. However, the fact that I worked at small companies allowed me to quickly build experience as well as confidence. More importantly, playing an integral part in different roles helped me become multi skilled and familiar with the work in different departments. I am sure your company will benefit from this. I've brought some references with me today to show you that my job performance at Agway was stellar.

Question: Then what is your biggest management weakness?

Answer: Sometimes I can get very impatient when people do not deliver work in a timely manner. To avoid feeling frustrated with co-workers, I've learned to establish clear deadlines and give friendly reminders a few days prior to keep projects on track.

Question: Tell me how you resolve conflicts in the office.

Answer: Conflicts are often the result of misunderstanding or miscommunication rather than any dispute or actual reasons. For example, in my last summer job, conflict occurred between two co-workers in my office. One of them often waited until the last minute to get his work done. The other who always worked more steadily and efficiently complained that she had missed more work and felt very uncomfortable with having to collaborate with him. As the mediator, I first asked the employees in conflict to talk about their problems. I empathized with both of them, making it clear that I did not take sides. This alone made them feel better. After getting both employees to calm down and see thing with less emotion, I asked them to describe how the other might be feeling and thinking and how the situation might look to the other party. Finally, I asked them to agree on a solution so that they could collaborate well by adjusting their work style. In short, I think the best way to resolve conflicts in office is treating employees with respect and empathy and making them communicate with logic and reason.

(Continued)

> **Question:** Well then, we'd love to have you come in and meet with a few of our department heads and wanted to know how much you're expecting to make at this job?
>
> **Answer:** I would need to learn more about the specific duties required of this position, which I look forward to learning more about in this interview. However, I do understand that positions similar to this one pay in the range of $40K to $60K in our region. With my experience, skills, and certifications, I would expect to receive something in the range of $45K to $50K.

IV Interview skills

Creating a compelling elevator pitch (self-introduction)

During job interviews, when you're asked "Tell me about yourself", you should be able to summarize who you are, what you do, and why you would be a perfect match within one minute or so. We also call this 'the elevator pitch', a short speech which helps you share your expertise and credentials quickly and effectively with people who don't know you. You can also use your elevator pitch to introduce yourself at networking events, professional association programs, or any other type of gathering.

Your self-introduction should be brief (30~60 seconds) and persuasive enough to spark the interviewer's interest in your background. Here is the outline for a powerful self-introduction.

(1) Who am I? (A brief personal information)

• Your name, your school, and what you're studying (For college students)

• Your name, field or industry you are in, your current position or employer (For professionals)

(2) What are my Unique Selling Points (UPS)? (Highlights of your qualifications)

• A statement that shows off your strengths and gives a little sense of your personality.

• 2~4 specific strengths or accomplishments that prove you meet or exceed the requirements.

• Anything about your personality that is applicable to the job (leader, team player, enjoy research, etc.).

(3) Why am I here? (Reasons why you have applied)

• Career objective or the type of position you want, interest in the company or what you can contribute.

Remember, this outline is just the starting point of your elevator speech. Use it to help inspire your own answer and be sure to tailor your self-introduction to particular situations.

The following pairs of examples show what sentences are more powerful for an elevator speech.

e.g. Weak: Hey, I'm Tochi, a human resources professional working for a bank. I am hard-working and accomplished.

Better: Hey, I'm Tochi, I'm a human resource professional with 8 years of experience managing all aspects of the HR function. I have a strong track record in helping to identify and recruit top-level talent into management.

Weak: My name is Justine. I am studying Finance at XYZ University. I expect to graduate this summer. My favorite courses are Macroeconomics, Microeconomics and Financial and managerial accounting.

Better: My name is Justine. I am a Finance major at XYZ University who has spent three years gaining experience and improving my skills in accounting and financial services.

Weak: In the past six years I served as a customer service manager at Megacompany Inc. responsible for managing the customer service team and handling customer service issues.

Better: I have spent the last six years developing my skills as a customer service manager for Megacompany Inc., where I have won several performance awards and been promoted twice. I love managing teams and solving customer problems.

Task 5. Read two elevator speeches below. Arrange the sentences in the right order according to the outline given below. Discuss in pairs: What components are included in the responses? Are they impressive enough to make the candidate stand out from others?

A	B
(1) In my current role at ABC, I have achieved an average of 12% sales growth over 3 years, consistently exceeding sales target. My strong networking skills have resulted in expanding our customer base by 8%.	(1) This year I interned at a public affairs consultancy and was fortunate to contribute to a high-profile campaign, enabling me to consolidate my research and analysis skills.
(2) Your company is among the top 10 fastest-growing companies in China, and I am very eager to meet the challenges of developing new territories for your company.	(2) One of the things I've enjoyed about university is the chance to broaden my horizons and try new things.
(3) I respond quite well under pressure and I am willing to go the extra mile to accomplish team goals. I am very confident that I match your current requirements.	(3) I'm in my final year at X University studying politics which has given me a unique opportunity to understand and analyse motivations of groups and individuals and be aware of my responsibilities as an active citizen.
(4) I graduated from X College with a bachelor's degree in Marketing and Finance. Since graduating from college, I have worked in sales for ABC Company for the last 6 years.	(4) This experience affirmed my desire to pursue a career in this field, which is why I'm sitting here today.

Task 6. Based on what you have learned about the strategies for creating a compelling self-introduction, write a well-thought-out elevator pitch for your job interview. The following outline may help you organize the content of your speech.

Greeting	Hello, my name is…
Education	I am a (sophomore, junior, etc.)…majoring in…
Experience	I have done (research, projects, etc.) on…/ I interned at…/ I am currently working in…
Accomplishments	I have (produced, presented, written) / I use my…skills / I learned…/ I improved…skills
Seeking	I am seeking a(n)…(internship, full-time job, etc.) / I'm interested in…company because I can…
Closing	That's why I'm here / I apply for this position. I know your company…, can you tell me a little bit about…?

This outline is just the starting point of your elevator speech. Use it to help inspire your own answer and be sure to tailor your self-introduction to particular situations.

Using STAR method to answer behavioral questions

A behavioral question is a question that aims at learning about your past "behaviors" in specific work situations. The prospective employer views your past behavior as an indicator of your future behavior. The key to answering such questions is telling "success stories" using the STAR method (Situation–Task–Action–Result). It is considered an effective way to demonstrate how you apply your working style, skills and knowledge to a range of career experiences. The method is also known as **CAR interview technique** (Context–Action–Result).

The STAR response strategy

The STAR method helps you to structure your response and talk about your positive characteristics. Here's how it works:

S = Situation: Describe a specific situation you were in. This situation can be from a previous job, from a volunteer experience, any relevant event. Be sure to give enough detail for the interviewer to understand (who, what, where, when, how).

T = Task: Describe the task you had to complete highlighting any specific challenges or constraint (e.g. deadlines, costs, other issues). Keep it specific but concise.

A = Action: Describe the specific actions you took to complete the task, incorporating skills that the interviewers are seeking (initiative, teamwork, leadership, dedication, etc.). Be sure to keep the focus on you. Even if you are discussing a group project or effort, describe what you did–not the efforts of the team.

R = Result: Describe the results of your experience. Quantify the results you achieved if possible and relate the skills accomplishments to the needs of the organization.

Task 7. Read the following interview answer. Identify the function of each sentence(s). Write the letter S, T, A or R next to each sentence.

Behavioral Question: Give an example of how you worked on a team.

Answer:

During my last semester in college, we were set a group task during our English course. _____

The task was to write a report about the development of language in Europe in the Middle Ages and present this to the class. _____

As team leader, I allocated sections to each person and set a deadline. I suggested that we meet independently before our weekly meeting to discuss our progress, and help each other out if we were having any difficulties. When we finished writing, we collated the report and I assigned each person a role for the presentation _____

Because of this structure, we were able to give a clear and professional presentation and received an A for the project. The professor really appreciated the way we worked together. _____

Task 8. Choose 2~3 common behavioral interview questions related to the following categories: teamwork, problem-solving, initiative / leadership, interpersonal skills, and challenge / stress / pressure. Determine what examples or success stories you have would be appropriate for the position based on its job description. Write your response to the question using the STAR method.

Skill	Your example / story
Teamwork	Situation: Task: Action: Result:
Problem-solving	Situation: Task: Action: Result:
_____ (Choose a skill)	Situation: Task: Action: Result:

Handling negative points

1. Be prepared to talk about aspects of your background that may be interpreted as negative, for example, low grade point average, no related work experience. Convince the recruiter of the positive attributes that can be found in these seemingly negative points by thinking about what compensating experience you may have.

For example, a low GPA could stem from having to fully support yourself through college.

eg. "I managed to maintain a 2.4 GPA while working 24 hours a week, and being active in two student groups."

You might have no related work experience, but plenty of experience that shows you to be a loyal and valued employee.

eg. "While working on the projects of my supervisor, I learned teamwork, appreciation, understanding, and sometimes, compromise."

2. If you are asked "What is your greatest weaknesses?", take the following steps to formulate your answer:

(1) Carefully consider one or two weaknesses you know you have had and have overcome: Remember, this weakness should not be a part of your personality that is very difficult to change. Don't pick a weakness that would disqualify you for the job, even if you have overcome it. You'd better choose weaknesses that are neutral or may be considered strengths when carried to an extreme.

eg. getting sressed around deadlines, being too critical of yourself or too result-driven.

(2) Explain how you want to improve yourself or how you have overcome your weaknesses.

e.g. "At university I found cross cultural communication skills difficult, particularly the differences between Europe, America and Asia. So I took a course on effective communication techniques to give me a good background on different cultural practices."

V Exercises and Practice

Answering interview questions

Task 9. Complete the interview answers by choosing the correct word in the bracket.

1. Question: Tell me about yourself.

(1) I will be receiving my BA _____ (in / of) Accounting from the University of Illinois and have already completed two internships with large public accounting firms in the _____ (passed / past) two summers. During my internship with XYZ Corporation, I was able to

successfully _____ (use / apply) what I learned in the classroom to my work assignments. My education and my internships have _____ (made / prepared) myself to become a world class accountant. I also earned the Intern of the Year _____ (Award / Reward) for the Chicago branch of KPMG this past summer. Everything I've read about your company and this position has only _____ (fulfilled / reinforced) my desire to work here. I believe I have what it takes to be successful in this position.

(2) I've _____ (worked / been working) as an administrative assistant for three years. At my _____ (current / existing) job in the finance department of a midsize company, I handle scheduling, meeting and travel planning for four executives and 20 staff members. I also help prepare correspondence, presentations and reports. I'm _____ (known for / longing for) being a detail-oriented, well-organized team player. I never _____ (meet / miss) deadlines. In my performance reviews, my supervisor always notes that he _____ (appreciates / appraises) my professionalism and enthusiasm for the job. With this experience under my belt, I'm looking for an opportunity in an organization like yours that works to improve the environment, which is something I'm _____ (cared / passionate) about.

(3) Hi, my name is Jin Xia and I am a sophomore _____ (major / majoring) in Biological Engineering. I am currently working in the laboratory of Dr. Lin, where our research is _____ (focused / concerned) on correcting mutations that cause orphan diseases. While my research is in the early stage, I have successfully _____ (announced / demonstrated) that the CRISPR technology method works in my hands. I plan to combine this experience working with DNA sequences with the knowledge that I have _____ (learned / gained) in my computer science courses, to contribute to the field of computational biology.

2. Question: Why do you want this job?

(1) This job is a good _____ (call / fit) for what I've been doing and enjoying throughout my career. It offers a _____ (opportunity / mix) of short-term projects and long-term goals. My organizational skills allow me to successfully multitask and complete both kinds of projects.

(2) I want this job because it _____ (emphasizes / focuses) sales and marketing, two of my greatest skill sets. In my _____ (current / previous) job, I increased sales by 15 percent. I know I could bring my ten years of sales and marketing experience to this company, and help you continue your years of _____ (increase / growth).

3. Question: What is your greatest strength?

(1) I think one of my strengths is my ability to _____ (maintain / learn) independently. I taught myself to use WordPress using YouTube videos, and now I singlehandedly run my organization's blog.

(2) I have an extremely strong work _____ (ethnic / ethic). When I'm working on a project, I don't just want to meet deadlines. Rather, I prefer to complete the project to the highest _____

(criterion / standard) well ahead of schedule. Last year, I even earned a _____ (fund / bonus) for completing my three most recent reports one week ahead of time.

4. Question: What's your greatest weakness?

(1) _____ (Sometimes / Occasionally) I struggle to focus on my duties. _____ (Therefore / However), I practice every day, trying to eliminate useless thoughts, and my concentration has _____ (progressed / improved) over the years. I still continue working _____ (on / about) it though, trying to eliminate distractions in work.

(2) When I started my college, I had _____ (trouble / preference) with procrastination, preferring to finish my task at the last minute. I found that it put me under unnecessary stress. _____ (Luckily / Unfortunately), I realized the problem quickly. _____ (As / Since) taking a time management course recently, I've _____ (identified / learnt) how to manage my schedule more effectively. Now procrastination is no longer a problem for me.

5. Question: Why should we hire you?

(1) Based on what you've said and from the research I've done, your company is looking for an administrative assistant who is both strong in interpersonal skills and in tech skills. I believe my experience _____ (aligns / relates) well with that and makes me a great _____ (value / fit). I am an effective communicator who is _____ (excellent / skilled) in giving oral presentations and communicating via email.

(2) I think that my experience with technology and, in particular, my ability to maintain and update websites, make me a good _____ (employee / match) for this position. In my most _____ (current / recent) position, I was _____ (charge / responsible) for maintaining our department web page. This _____ (asks / required) updating student and faculty profiles, and posting information about upcoming events. I loved this work. In my free time, I learned to code in JavaScript and Swift. I then used my coding skills to revamp our homepage and received praise from our department head for my _____ (initiative / commitment).

6. Question: Why do you choose our company?

(1) I have used your software products for many years, and always been very _____ (amazed / impressed) with the innovations and consistent concern for helping your customers learn how to use them effectively. I would greatly enjoy helping you to continue to innovate and to _____ (increase / achieve) your market share."

(2) Your business is known for making a _____ (commitment / difference) to bettering the community. Your company also has a good _____ (reputation / vision) in the industry for innovative thinking and taking serious corporate responsibility for the society. I would love the opportunity to use my 10 years of experience in advertising to make a significant contribution to its goals.

7. Question: What are your goals in five years time?

(1) My long-term goals involve _____ (contributing / growing) with a company where I can continue to learn, take on additional _____ (responsibilities / function), and contribute as much value as possible to the team. I love that your company emphasizes professional development opportunities. I would take full advantage of the educational resources available.

(2) I see the next few years in this company as an _____ (platform / opportunity) to gain skills and experience. _____ (While / Once) I gain enough experience, I would like to move on from a technical position to management. However, for now, I am excited about focusing on and applying my technical skills in this job.

Communicating in a job interview

Task 10. Translate the following sentences into English.

(1) 久闻贵公司大名。
_____

(2) 你们能把我列入考虑，我觉得很荣幸。
_____

(3) 我应征这个职位最有价值的技能是精通法语。
_____

(4) 在学校我一直名列前茅。
_____

(5) 我有十年的工作经验，还获得了硕士学位，非常适合这个职位的要求。
_____

(6) 我起初担任初级工程师，后来一路升任高级工程师。
_____

(7) 同事对我的工作效率印象深刻。
_____

(8) 我认为可靠是我的最优秀的特质之一。
_____

(9) 尾巴工作做好，我愿意额外付出。
_____

(10) 我何时可以得到确定的通知？
_____

Assignments

1. Rehearsed interview.

Compose responses to likely interview questions and then practice by speaking aloud by yourself, enabling you to hear how your answers sound and adjust your verbiage as needed. You can record these rehearsals and then listen to the recordings from the employer's perspective. You can also try rehearsing in front of a mirror to check out your nonverbal mannerisms.

2. Mock interview.

Work in groups of 3. Take turns playing the role of the employer, the job candidate, or the observer. Evaluate the candidate's qualifications for the position and make comments.

PART TWO
STARTING A JOB

Unit 4 Workplace correspondence: Overview

Workplace writing is the most common type of writing outside of school. When you graduate and enter the workforce, you will find good writing skills are a key asset at every stage of their career. Correspondence is the means through which we exchange our ideas, thoughts and other information in the workplace. This unit will give an overview of workplace writing, providing instruction in planning, organizing, and writing effective workplace correspondence such as letters, memos, and E-mail messages.

Objectives

After completing this unit, you will be able to
◆ Understand the process of writing a workplace document;
◆ Discuss how letters, memos, and e-mail messages differ in format;
◆ Explain how Audience, Purpose, Style, and Tone shape each workplace correspondence;
◆ Analyze audience needs in specific workplace situations;
◆ Identify common types of workplace correspondence and understand their features;
◆ Identify and select appropriate style and tone for common workplace correspondence.

I Pre-class activities

Research and Explore

Task 1. Do preliminary research on the following questions and get prepared for class discussion.

(1) What are the differences between general writing and workplace writing?

_____
_____
_____

(2) Identify a job you may like to have in the future. What types of workplace documents do you think a person in this job might need to write? What are the key considerations for planning and writing these documents?

_____

_____

_____

📢 Case study

The Broaster Company purchased ten computers from Supreme Computer Co., Ltd. However, they find the products unsatisfactory. The following documents are series of correspondence written to different audiences for different purposes using different media.

Task 2. Read the following documents and give a brief report based on your answers to the following questions:

(1) What is the relationship between the writer and the recipient of the letter, email and the memo respectively?

How does the intended audience influence the choice of words and the tone in a document?

(2) Why does the writer use letter instead of email or memo to make a serious complaint to a company?

In what situations will a writer choose to send a letter, an email and a memo respectively?

(3) When is it appropriate to write in a formal tone? In a casual tone?

(4) How are letters, emails and memos similar or different? Summarize the differences between them. Look in particular at the purpose, the intended reader, the format, the length, the opening and closing of the messages, and the formality of the language.

① **Business letter**

The Broaster Company, LLC
23 Massachusetts Avenue, NW
Washington, CD 20001
(202)222-2190
www.broaster.com

July 27, 2015

Mr. David Harris
Supreme Computer Co., Ltd
1636 Bladensburg Rd. NE
Washington D.C. 20002

Re: Defective computers complaint

Dear Mr. Harris:

I am writing this letter regarding the computers that we purchased from your company on June 18. Its order number is ORD-441135. After limited use of your computers, however, we have had the following problems:

Unit 4 Workplace correspondence: Overview

(Continued)

- Two notebook computers wouldn't boot up.
- One monitor made a continuous, high-pitched whining sound.
- Two desktop computers came infected with viruses.

We have already attempted to resolve this problem by calling upon your technicians to repair the computers On July 2nd. Unfortunately, the problem remains unresolved.

Because of the number of problems, we do not have the confidence in any of the equipment you installed. As a result, we're returning them to you today and requesting a full refund according to your warranty.

I look forward to your written reply and resolution to this issue. Please respond within 7 days of the receipt of this letter. I have prepared a complaint for submission to the proper agencies for investigation. I will not file the complaint if you resolve the problem within this time period I have indicated.

Thank you for your anticipated assistance in resolving my problem. Please contact me at 501-683-2255 or by email at stephen-powers@ broaster.com.

Sincerely,

Stephen Powers

Stephen Powers
Purchasing Manager

Enc: Purchase contract

② **E-mail**

From: "Dan Smith" <dan-smith@broaster.com >
To: Stephen Powers <stephen-powers@ broaster.com >
Subject: Computer Problems
Date: Mon, 27 July 2015 08:59:32 -0500

Hi Steve:

On May 18, we bought 10 computers from the Supreme Computer Co., Ltd. Unfortunately, their products haven't performed well. The major problems include:
1) Two notebook computers won't boot up.
2) One monitor continues to make a high-pitched whining sound.
3) Two desktop computers came infected with viruses.

These problems remain unsolved after their technicians came to our office to do repair work on July 2nd. I feel that we should consider sending these computers back and get new ones from another supplier. I don't feel confident with any equipment from this supplier.

Attached is our original purchase contract with Supreme Computer Company in Microsoft Word 97 format.

Thanks,

Dan

③ **Memo**

Memorandum

To: Dan Smith
From: Gorge Martin
Date: July 26, 2015
Re: Computer problems

We are still having problems with the five new computers we have purchased from David Harris at the Supreme Computer Co., Ltd. The problems we have been having include:

1) Two notebook computers won't boot up.
2) One monitor continues to make a high-pitched whining sound.
3) Two desktop computers came infected with viruses.

Could you ask their technicians to fix these problems asap? Thanks.

II Introduction

Writing is an essential job-related skill. You will spend a fair amount of time at work communicating ideas through writing. Business correspondence is a written message which deals with business matters. Whether you are writing a letter to your client, emailing a response to a colleague's question, or issuing a memo about the company policy, your writing ability can enhance or hinder your career success to some extent.

However, you may find it hard to transfer your academic writing skills to workplace because workplace writing and college writing are different. Writing at work focuses on completing a job-related task whereas academic writing is intended to demonstrate your knowledge of a topic or thesis and to express your opinions. Unlike academic writing where you write complex sentences and lengthy paragraphs to develop the complexity of your ideas, workplace writers typically write shorter, simpler sentences and include much less paragraphs. More importantly, work-related writing targets multiple audiences with different perspectives. In college your primarily write to your instructor. Therefore, as a fresh graduate or a new hire, you must better the written communication skills needed to succeed in the workplace.

Types of workplace correspondence

Letters, email and memos are common types of **workplace correspondence** you'll come across in the standard business or government settings. As the basic written genres, letters, emails, and memos serves different purposes. They can be **internal or external written communication**.

Unit 4 Workplace correspondence: Overview

Internal written communication refers to day-to-day exchanges among employers and employees at all levels of the organization. External communication includes communication with outsiders of the writer's organization, such as customers, suppliers, media, governmental agencies, other businesses, etc.. To write effective letters, emails, and memos, you need to learn some specific conventions of layout and style appropriate to organizations, but you should also continually develop your workplace writing skills.

Genre type	Format
Business / Professional Letters • Letters remain the most formal and polished genre option for workplace communication. They are typically suited for important messages such as proposals, inquires, agreements, and recommendations. • Business letters are used to communicate with individuals outside of the office (customers, colleagues in other businesses, service providers, government officials and job applicants, etc.). • They may be also used in formal communication within an organization or for official personnel records (contracts, annual job evaluations / reviews).	Date (Month Day, Year) Mr/Ms Full name of recipient. Title/Position of Recipient. Company Name Recipient's Address Line 1 Recipient's Address Line 2 Dear Ms./Mrs./Mr. Last Name: Subject: Title of Subject Body Paragraph 1 ... Body Paragraph 2 ... Body Paragraph 3 ... Sincerely Signature Your Name Your Title
E-mail • Most writing in the workplace now involves this quick and convenient form of communication. • E-mails are good for variable audiences. They can be directed to individuals and groups of any size, internal and external recipients. • E-mails allow for attachments and links, so you can share longer, more detailed documents with readers. • This is a medium for formal notices and updates, as well as informal exchanges.	From: Samuel Allison <samuel.allison@xyz-inc.com> To: Karen Jones <karen.jones@lmno-inc.com> Subject: Marks report salutation — Dear Karen: Message Content — Have you completed a revision of the Marks report, and if so, may I have a copy of it? I would like to take it to my meeting with Rachel tomorrow. I will be in my office until noon if you have any questions. Closing — Regards, Sam Signature File — Samuel Allison Director, Marketing XYZ, Inc. 123 Anywhere Street New York, NY 10024 Tel: (212) 555-1234 Fax: (212) 555-3456 samuel.allison@xyz-inc.com www.xyz-inc.com Body
Memos • Memos follow emails as a convenient, quick genre for routine workplace messages, usually used for short internal communications. • Memos are used for sharing short reports and proposals or for communicating current projects, company's problems and solutions or changes in business procedures or other internal topics. • Memos can be shared as email attachments or distributed in print. Usually important and lengthy documents that require close scrutiny may be printed as a hard copy memorandum.	[Company Name] **Memo** To: [Recipient Name] From: [Your Name] cc: [Name] Date: [Click to select date] Re: [Subject] [Type memo here]

(Continued)

Genre type	Format
Text messages / Texting Text messaging for your business is a convenient, effective, and simple tool. It may be sent to your boss, team members, colleagues or customers when a phone call would be impolite or inappropriate. Sending and receiving text messages for business is becoming increasingly popular, creating more opportunities for your business to engage customers and prospects.	Messages screen showing: 9:32AM — Nick, I sent our proposal this morning via email. We look forward to working with you on this project. - Sam 9:35AM — We received the document and are reviewing the terms. We are going to need a few extra days. How soon do you need an answer?

Task 3. Read sample documents in Task 2 and the correspondence you have collected and complete the following table about the differences between letters, emails, and memos.

Points of difference	Letter	Email	Memo
Reader	External, internal sometimes		
Degree of formality			
Components / Format		From, To, Subject Salutation, message, complimentary close, signature	
Length	Comparatively long		

Writing process

There are 3 stages involved in every workplace writing: plan, draft, and revise. The following figure shows a three-step writing process which helps business writers and professionals create effective messages in any medium. If you learn to internalize the 3 steps of the writing process, you will likely produce effective workplace documents. These stages are not necessarily linear and often overlap one another.

• **Planning:** You identify everything you need to do before starting your rough draft. Audience, purpose and channel of communication should be considered at this point.

• **Drafting:** You create your initial draft by structuring and outlining your ideas in an organized way to convey a particular idea while making the tone, style, and content appropriate for the intended audience.

• **Revising:** You review, modify, and improve the draft by reorganizing content, editing to improve clarity, style and readability, and proofreading and correcting errors in grammar and mechanics.

Unit 4 Workplace correspondence: Overview

1. Plan
- Determine the purpose
- Analyze the audience (relatipnship, needs, background, reaction, etc.)
- Choose the channel of communication (letter, email, memo, etc.)

2. Draft
- Gather and organize information
  — Define the main idea — Limit the scope
  — Chose the direct or indirect approach
  — Chosse an organizational structure
- Select style and tone
- Use the appropriate strategies (reader-centered)

3. Revise
- Revise the message
- Edit (clarity, conciseness, tone, readablitiy)
- Proofread (spelling, grammar, punctuation, format)

1. Planning

(1) Determine the purpose

Workplace documents must have a clear purpose. Defining your purpose will set the tone, the style, and structure of your writing right at the very beginning so that you can adapt the message to your purpose. Business writing aims to serve any one of many purposes. Here are just a few purposes of business writing:

Purpose analysis	Writing tips
Why are you writing? • What is your primary purpose? • What is your secondary purpose? What are your expected actions or outcomes?	• Make your primary purpose the main idea of the message and use supporting details to convey your secondary purpose. • Place the main point in the right position depending on the message and the audience.
Purposes may be to: • inform • persuade • build goodwill • request or inquire • instruct or direct action • record and document • propose or recommend	Main point in the opening paragraph e.g. • *This report summarized the results of the first-quarter sales.* • *You are invited to help us celebrate 20 years of automotive service to the residents of Monroe County.* Main point in the middle paragraph e.g. • *Thank you for your interested in our latest products... Unfortunately, the latest Ipod is currently unavailable in our store.*

(2) Analyze the audience

Audiences tend to be interested in messages that relate to their needs, interests, goals, and motivations. To communicate effectively, you have to know your audience before you begin writing, since you will need to adapt your writing to fit the people you expect to read. You should try to picture the typical reader in your mind and develop an audience profile for your message and write up accordingly.

Audience analysis		Writing tips
Relationship to you	• What is the audience's relationship to you? *internal or external to the organization* *downward, upward, horizontal* (superior to subordinate, subordinate to superior, between coworkers)	• Determine the correct **writing channel** *letter / email for external communication* *email / memo for internal communication* • Use the appropriate **style & tone** *formal, conversational, informal* *courteous, friendly, sincere*
Knowledge / Experience	• What is the level of audience's education, expertise and vocabulary? *Expert / specialist, executive / technician, layperson / customer* • What do they already know about this topic?	• Write at the appropriate **level of language** *technical terms / scientific vocabulary or lay language / jargon-free vocabulary* • Complete and detailed information or a concise outline
Needs / Interests / Expectations	• What do they need to know about this topic? • What do they expect from that document? • What is their reason for reading my work?	• Write from the **audience's point of view** • Focus on their needs (*timing, cost, details*) • Emphasize benefits to the audience
Demographics	• Age, gender, location, education, income, marital status, cultural background, values, language, etc.?	• Adapt the message to their culture • Avoid potentially offensive expressions (sexist, racist, pompous language)
Attitudes / Emotional reactions	• What is their attitude to you and your work? • What is their potential reaction to the message? *Positive, negative or neutral?* *Happy, angry, hostile, skeptical, or resistant?*	• Use the appropriate **approach and tone** to convey the message *Approach – direct or indirect* *Tone – positive, friendly tone*

(3) Choose the right communication channel

It is important to select the medium that is most appropriate for the objective and target audience of the message. There are five factors to consider before choosing a communication channel.

• Formality: the degree of formality of your message and format.

• Confidentiality: the secure form of communication for highly important and sensitive information.

• Permanent record: the necessity of requiring the permanent record.

- Signatures: the necessity to verify the identity of the writer.
- Urgency: how urgent you need to get your message out.
- Speed: the speed of delivery and feedback required.
- Length: the length of the message (more than one computer screen).

For example, in Case Studies of Section I, the manager chooses to write a formal complaint letter with his signature and the original purchase contract enclosure, conveying more formality and seriousness than email or memo messages.

2. Drafting

(1) Generate and organize information

With purpose and audience in mind, you need to organize information clearly and effectively.

- Brainstorm and record all ideas that come to mind about the topic. Brainstorming methods include: 5W questions (Who / What / Where / When / Why / How) and a mind map of the main concepts, sub-concepts and minor concepts.o
- Determine what is the main idea of the message and choose an approach for stating the main idea depending on whether the main idea is good, bad or neutral news. (Direct vs. Indirect approach)

Direct approach – Start with the main point or good news followed by details or explanation. It applies to most positive and neutral messages (good news, routine, etc.). A message organized this way saves the reader time by getting to the purpose of the message right away.	**Indirect approach** – Put the reasons, details or explanation first (buffer or cushion), then the bad news. Negative messages (bad news, refusal, unfavorable decision, etc.) usually use the indirect approach to help the receiver understand and accept the messages. The goal is to minimize any negative reaction your reader may have.
This is just a quick note to tell you that our whole department is excited about your decision to accept our offer of employment. We couldn't be happier to welcome you to the team. (Opening: Good news) As we agreed, your first day on the new job is Tuesday, May 8. We'll expect you at 9 a.m. FYI, the dress code here is business casual. You will meet your new employee mentor, Paul Smith when you come in on Tuesday. He'll help you get to know the company and your new department. (Middle: Explanation or details) If you have questions, please feel free to email or call me. My number is 910-244-3256. We really look forward to working with you. (Closing: Goodwill or restate)	Thank you for your interest in our company. (Opening: Buffer or cushion) As you know, we interviewed a number of candidates for the Product Manager position, and we have determined that several other candidates we interviewed have more experience that is directly relevant to the requirements of our job opening. (Middle: Explanation or reasons) This letter is to let you know that you have not been selected for the position. (Middle: Bad news) Thank you for taking the time to come to EPMC to meet our interview team. You are kindly encouraged to apply again in the future if we post a job opening for which you qualify. (Closing: Goodwill or restate)

• Choose an organizational structure

> ✧ **Importance / Inverted pyramid structure** Begin with the most important message.
> ✧ **Problems-solution structure** Begin with the description of the problems, and then the solution to these problems.
> ✧ **Chronological structure** Present information in in order of time.
> ✧ **Topic structure** Arrange information by topics or subheadings.
> ✧ **General-to-specific structure** Begin with a general idea followed by supporting information.
> ✧ **Specific-to-general structure** Begin with details followed by a general idea.

(2) Select the style and tone

Style

Style is made up of the words and sentences that a writer chooses in order to produce a desired response in the readers. A writer needs to present the information in an easy-to-understand manner through the appropriate choice of words, grammar, sentence length and type.

An important part of workplace writing style is its **degree of formality**. Workplace writing varies from the conversational style often found in personal email messages to the more formal, legalistic style found in contracts. A style between these two extremes is appropriate for the majority of correspondence: memos, emails, and letters. The scale of formality is shown in the graph below.

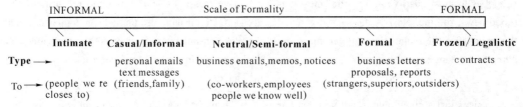

As a general rule, writing for professional purposes is likely to require the formal style, and individual communications can use the informal style; external communication is more formal than internal communication; and upward communication is more formal than lateral or downward communication. Formal language usually conveys respect, politeness and distance while informal language conveys familiarity and friendliness.

Tone

Tone refers to the writer's mood, feelings and attitude toward the subject and the reader of the message. The overall tone of workplace correspondence should be confident, courteous, positive, and professional in order to have the message well received. Although business writing is generally becoming more informal and straightforward, you still need to use your judgment to find the right tone depending on the purpose, the audience, and the content of correspondence you are writing. Ultimately, the best approach is to put yourself in your readers' place and consider the message from their viewpoint.

For example, in the Case Study of Section I, the complaint letter written to the computer company sounds firm and serious since the computers were of poor qualities and had caused trouble for the users. On the other hand, the memo sent to the colleague about the computer uses more conversational and friendly tone.

Compare the tones used in the sentences below:

• *You have to finish the project by the day after tomorrow. If you fail in doing so, we might lose the client and that will not be good for us!*

• *Richard, this client is important to us, and we cannot afford to lose this account. This project needs to be completed by the day after tomorrow; hence, we are assigning it to you. Please let us know if you want any further details.*

III Writing skills

Using the appropriate style and tone

Using the appropriate style and tone can help the writer communicate the desired message and achieve the desired results. When deciding which style is appropriate to your message you, consider the following factors: the particular type of document, the reader's needs and expectation, and the purpose and situation. Whichever style you write in – formal or informal – be sure to keep it consistent, do not mix the two.

There are a number of ways to convey degrees of formality in writing, including:

• the choice of words, phrases and expressions
• the use of contractions
• the use of specific grammar structures e.g., the passive voice
• the sentence length and structure

Formal	Semi-formal / Neutral	Informal
Use formal and big words	Use simple and common words	Use more colloquialisms
e.g. The economy is *currently* quite robust; *nevertheless*, some specialists *predict* an *imminent* recession.	e.g. The economy is very *strong right now, but* some specialists say we'll have a recession soon.	e.g. *kids, guy, awesome, a lot, I mean, How come?*
Avoid slang, idioms, text speak	Avoid slang, text speak; may use idiom	Use slang, text speak frequently
e.g. The software is *quite user-friendly*. A million *dollars* in profit	e.g. The software is *easy to use* A million *dollars* in profit Thanks, and we look forward to meeting you	e.g. The software is *a piece of cake*. A million *bucks* in profit Tks & we look 4ward 2 meeting u.

(Continued)

Formal	Semi-formal / Neutral	Informal
Avoid phrasal verbs	May use phrasal verbs	
e.g. The client *requested* a contract. We will *reduce* spending.	e.g. The client *asked for* a contract. We will *cut down on* spending.	
Avoid contractions	May use contractions	Use contractions
e.g. The shipment *has not* arrived. *We would* like to inform you...	e.g. The shipment *hasn't* arrived. *We'd* like to inform you…	I'm, you're, can't, don't, wasn't, it's, won't, shouldn't
Avoid abbreviations; use full versions	May use abbreviations or full versions	Use abbreviations
e.g. The results have arrived from the *laboratory*.	e.g. The results have arrived from the *lab*.	e.g. *info, lab, veggie, pro, vet,* etc..
Use third person and passive voice	Use first person and active voice	Use active voice
e.g. It *has been notice*d that…	e.g. We *have noticed* that…	We *'ve noticed* that…
Longer and more complex sentences	Short and simple sentences	Ellipsis, fragments
e.g. *Research has shown that learning a second language, in addition to leading to expanded career and social opportunities, can also expand the reasoning capability of the brain, although this finding is disputed by some scientists.*	e.g. *Learning another language can improve your career and social life. Some people also say it can make you smarter, but others disagree. It is not a problem. I look forward to meeting you.*	e.g. *No problem Look forward to meeting you. Finished your work yet? Lots to tell you.*

Task 4. Read three pieces of correspondence. Discuss with your partner the level of formality of each correspondence. Explain your reasons and underline the word and expressions that make them formal, semi-formal or informal.

1

Judy,

Sorry but I can't make it on Friday. Didn't have time for it. Can we put the meeting off to the following week?

Regards,
Adam

2

Hello,

I read on your web site that you offer Music CD copying for large quantities of CDs. I'd like to inquire about the procedures involved in these services.

Are the files transferred online, or are the titles sent by CD to you by standard mail? How long does it usually take to produce approximately 500 copies? Are there any discounts on such a large quantity?

Thank you for taking the time to answer my questions. I look forward to your response.

Jack Finley

Unit 4 Workplace correspondence: Overview

3

Dear Mr. Parker,

I am writing this letter to acquaint you with my interest in being associated with your esteemed organization. I am pleased to present this proposal to your organization. It would be an honor to work with you.

We are into providing customer service support since the last 5 years. We have worked with various reputed names in this short span of time and provided the required support ensuring good quality.

We have heard about your products and services and are confident that we would be able to provide the required after-sales service to your clients. Our customer service executives are ready to help the customers at all times.

Request you to kindly consider our proposal and allow us to serve your customers.

Sincerely,

John Smith

Task 5. Select the appropriate style and tone for the following situations. Consider the purpose, audience and topic when choosing the tone. Two or more tones may apply.

> formal, informal, appreciative, friendly, firm, courteous, regretful, enthusiastic, confident direct, indirect, humble, warm

(1) Applying for a job position   _____

(2) Declining a job offer   _____

(3) Accepting a job offer   _____

(4) Asking a coworker to send the information   _____

(5) Asking a superior to send the information   _____

(6) Apologizing to a customer for a mistake   _____

(7) Congratulating an employee on an accomplishment   _____

(8) Reprimanding an employee   _____

Task 6. Read the following sentences that appear in different types of documents and decide whether the tone and degree of formality is appropriate for the given situation.

(1) **a cover letter accompanying your resume:** Here's my resume.

(2) **an email message to a superior:** You need to stay until the banquet ends, which will be around 5 p.m. tomorrow.

(3) **a complaint response letter to a customer:** We regret any inconvenience you have experienced, and we assure you that we are anxious to retain you as a satisfied customer.

(4) **an email message to a friend:** Call me back ASAP.

(5) **a note to the office cleaner:** I would appreciate it if you could kindly clean under my desk in a timely fashion.

(6) **an email message to the recruiter:** I am writing to inform you that I am unable to accept the position you offered.

(7) **a letter to your supplier:** We can't understand why you have had trouble with the goods.

Applying the principles of effective workplace writing

In workplace writing, you should put yourself in the reader's place and focus on the reader's needs, reactions, or interests. The key to successful communications is to make the reader feel in your letter, email, or memo that the most important person in our business relationship is YOU, the reader.

Generally speaking, all business writing must be clear and concise with simple, straightforward language. The table below indicates the 6 C's, the guidelines you can follow in workplace writing. The first C is related to reader-writer relationship and the other Cs are about language use.

The 6 C's principles boil down to You-attitude. You-attitude is more likely to motivate the reader to act towards your desired direction, make you appear more trustworthy, and promote a feel-good atmosphere. To come across as considerate and polite in your writing, you need to

• avoid any words or phrases that convey sense of superiority, impatience or anger;

• avoid any words or phrases that might offend or embarrass the reader;

• try to emphasize the benefits to the reader.

Writing tips	Examples

• **Courteous / Considerate:** Always put your reader first in order to build goodwill.
  Utilize a "you" attitude, focus on "you" instead of "I" or "we";
  Use positive words and tone. Emphasize positive, pleasant facts;
  Select gender-neutral language.
	(1) *Your package will be delivered as soon as possible after 23rd June.* **(Positive, courteous, You-attitude)** *We cannot deliver your package before 23rd June.*
	(2) *A good police officer knows his or her duty.* **(Gender-neutral)** *A good policeman knows his duty.*

• **Clear:** Make sure your intended meaning is clear to the reader.
  Use simple, understandable and plain language;
  Avoid ambiguity;
  Use bulleted lists to make key information easy to find;
  Use bold and italic to emphasize your point;
  Split information into paragraphs with one idea per paragraph.
	(1) *He knew the proposed policy would work.* **(Clear)** *He discerned that the promulgated policy would function.*
	(2) *The lawyer went off to court with her legal team to fight.* **(Unambiguous)** *The lawyer went off to court to fight with her legal team.*

Unit 4 Workplace correspondence: Overview

(Continued)

Writing tips	Examples
• **Concise:** Express your ideas in the fewest words. Avoid wordiness and unnecessary repetition; Avoid roundabout expressions. Use short and effective sentences; Use the active voice when you can; Get straight to the point.	(1) *offer assistance to* — *help* *combine together* — *combine* *Under circumstances in which* — *When* (2) *The team achieved its goals.* **(Concise and clear)** *Goals were achieved by the team.*
• **Concrete:** Convey message in precise terms. Use specific and precise words, avoid vague or abstract words; Provide facts, figures, statistics, and details.	1. Your shipment will arrive <u>by March 15</u>. **(Concrete)** Your shipment will arrive <u>soon</u>.
• **Correct:** Strive for accuracy in information as well as mechanics. Make sure your document has no grammar, spelling and punctuation errors; Make sure your document is in the correct format.	1. Mr. Sun <u>submit</u> the financial report to the Vice President, who <u>thought</u> that it <u>is</u> poorly formatted. **(Correct)** Please address the following issues: grant-writing principles, <u>avoiding</u> pitfalls when writing grant proposals, and <u>to get</u> potential funding sources.
• **Complete:** Include all the information the reader needs to have; Provide all necessary information; Answer all questions asked (or implied); Add something extra (when appropriate).	

Task 7. Review the 6 C's of workplace writing and compare the original sentences and revised sentences in the following table.

(1) What tone or attitude is conveyed by the original sentence? Which rule listed in six Cs is broken?

(2) What techniques does the writer use to revise the sentence for better communicative effect on the reader?

(**Techniques:** formal language, indirect approach, positive language, courteous and considerate (You-attitude), use gender-neutral language, concise language, clear and understandable words)

Original	Revised
It is the responsibility of our Production Department to see that it meets the requirements of our Sales Division.	Our Production Department must meet our Sales Division's requirements.
Your team didn't complete the project on time.	The project was not completed on time.

(Continued)

Original	Revised
A chairperson is supposed to represent his organization as its figurehead.	A chairperson is supposed to represent his or her organization as its figurehead.
Since we haven't written you for some time, please help us bring our records up-to-date by filling out and returning the other half of this card.	Please fill out and return the other half of this card so that dividend checks, premium notices and other messages of importance may reach you promptly.
I can't allow anyone in the organization to come late on a daily basis. I'm sorry that I can't give you the full-attendance bonus.	We encourage punctuality, and we urge you to be on time on a regular basis so that you can get your full-attendance bonus.
We regret to inform you that we are unable to give you the discount you requested. Our company has recently been affected very badly by the global slump in electronic sales.	Due to the recent global slump in sales, we regret to inform you that we are unable to give you the discount you requested.
It's hardly possible that our trigger could have misfired without some contributing cause; nevertheless, to help out those who lack technical know-how, a company as responsible as Creative Guns can gladly replace the trigger you have.	To prevent your gun from misfiring again, we will gladly replace the trigger you have.
Recommending that we work on a hospital employee relations improvement program is not something he would recommend.	He wouldn't recommend that we work on a program to improve relations among hospital employees.

Planning the message of workplace correspondence

Planning is a very vital step in workplace writing. It is necessary that all the key elements be taken into full consideration along with adequate emphasis on communication strategies.

Task 8. Look at the following situations and complete the following table. You need to:

• Analyze the audience and purpose of the communication;

• Decide on the appropriate channel of communication, degree of formality, tone, and the approach.

In some cases, more than one way of communication may be appropriate.

(1) An employee gives coworkers and managers an update on his work or provides regular progress report.

Unit 4　Workplace correspondence: Overview

(2) The HR manager notifies the new hire of his employment contract with the company and requires acknowledgement of receipt of the message with his handwritten signature.

(3) You are to write on behalf of the General Manager of your company to the Event Manager of a hotel to arrange a conference there.

(4) You want to inform your employer that you are resigning due to personal issues.

(5) The administrative assistant informs all staff of the company's annual picnic.

(6) The job candidate writes to the HR manager to decline a job offer.

(7) The director's office announces a company policy: Cell phones should not be used for surfing the internet or gaming during work hours.

	Audience (internal vs. external, relationship, reaction)	Purpose	Channel (by letter, email or memo)	Degree of formality (formal, neutral or informal)	Tone	Approach (direct or indirect)
1						
2						
3						
4						
5						
6						
7						

IV　Exercises and Practice

Understanding the degree of formality

Task 9. Read the following expressions and sentences and decide which is formal (F) and which is informal (I).

Functions	Expressions	Functions	Expressions
Salutation	Hi Peter	Requesting	Can you…?
	Dear Ms. Short		I was wondering if you could…?
Opening	I am writing in connection with…		I would appreciate it if you could
	Just a quick note to say…		I'd like to…
	I am delighted to inform you that…	Apologizing	I would like to apologize for…
	I regret to inform you that…		Sorry for
	With reference to your letter…	Inquiring	Could you clarify…?
Reference	I have received your letter of…		Would you happen to know…?
	Thank you for your email dated…		Do you know…?
Ending	I look forward to meeting you…	Urgency	You must / have to…
	Looking forward to meeting you		It is vital / essential / important that…
	Let me know if you need any more help.	Refusing	Unfortunately, we will not be able to…
	Do not hesitate to contact me if you require further assistance.		I can't… I would rather not…
Closing	All the best	Notification	I am writing to let you know that …
	Yours sincerely		Please be aware / informed that …

Writing clearly and concisely

Task 10. Replace the out-of-date or extremely formal expressions with clear, simple and familiar words.

Too formal expressions	Clear and familiar expressions
(1) Attached hereto please find your statement of account.	
(2) I am pleased to provide, pursuant to your request, the following information regarding the program.	
(3) Please be advised that the prices have increased.	
(4) This is to acquaint you with the fact that payment has been duly noted.	

Task 11. Replace the wordy expressions with concise expressions.

Wordy	Concise	Wordy	Concise
Prior to the event		In spite of the fact that	
At this point in time		Basic fundamentals	
Subsequent to		In the year of 2018	
In the event that		Merge together	
In view of the fact that		Mutual cooperation	
Until such time as		Long in length	
Because of the fact that		give assistance to	
Really excellent		have a discussion	

Task 12. Identify the wordy words in the sentences and rewrite each sentence to express simple or obvious ideas.

(1) **Wordy:** Because of the fact that many of the words in this sentence are basically unnecessary, it would really be a very good idea to edit the sentence for conciseness.
   Concise: _____

(2) **Wordy:** We have enclosed a report which shows further details of construction on page four.
   Concise: _____

(3) **Wordy:** In the event that going out for the purpose of shopping with them cannot be avoided, it is necessary that we first go to the bank, in light of the fact that I am out of cash.
   Concise: _____

(4) **Wordy:** There are twenty-five students who have already expressed a desire to attend the program next summer. It is a matter of the gravest importance to these students who gain the most by the government grant.
   Concise: _____

(5) **Wordy:** Mr. Stevens, who was our Chief Financial Officer, won his lawsuit.
   Concise: _____

Writing politely / Using positive language

Task 13. Change the negative statements to positive ones.

(1) Never fail to clean your work area before you leave each day.

_____

(2) Do not use negative words in your messages.

_____

(3) You cannot use the drive-through banking service before 9 a.m..

_____

(4) We will not exchange goods in bad condition.
_____

Task 14. Rewrite the following sentences to achieve You-attitude.
 e.g. *We-attitude: We provide health insurance to all employees.*
  You attitude: You receive health insurance as a full-time employee.

> You-attitude principles involve more than using "you" and "your"; it means seeing from the reader's viewpoint and seeing reader benefits, and writing accordingly.
> • Use "you" more often than "I" or "we" in positive situations.
> • Avoid "you" in delivering bad news. You can place emphasis on things, not people, and use passive voice.

(1) **We-Attitude:** I will issue two uniforms to you next Monday morning.
 You Attitude: _____
(2) **We-Attitude:** We allow a 2 percent discount if the bill is paid by the 10th of the month.
 You-Attitude: _____
(3) **We-attitude:** Obviously, you did not proofread the final copy of the contract.
 You-attitude: _____
(4) **We-attitude:** We believe our training courses can help employees become better communicators.
 You-attitude: _____

Assignments

1. Find a business document and conduct a genre analysis.

  Look for an example of business correspondence, such as a promotional business letter or email message you received, or a memo from your boss or supervisor. Analyze each document by answering the following questions:

 • What is the genre of the document (letter, email, report, flier, manual, etc.)?
 • What is the document's purpose(s)?
 • Who is the primary reader of the documents? Are there are also secondary readers?
 • Describe and comment on the layout and content organization.
 • Describe the characteristics of the language (level of formality, style and tone).

  Share your example and the analysis with your classmates.

Unit 4 Workplace correspondence: Overview

2. Think of a topic and practice adopting the audience-centered approach.

Audience awareness is one of the keys to effective writing. Think of a specific topic and two specific kinds of audiences. Consider how the intended audience will influence the choice of words and use of language. Then write a short example of how this topic might be presented to each of the two audiences.

_____

_____

_____

Unit 5 Professional Letters

Professional letters are a written form of communication that convey important information to someone outside of your organization. Despite the popularity of emails and text messages, organizations and government departments still rely on professional letters as a strong official medium of communication. This unit will teach you how to plan and create professional letters. It will introduce the professional letter formats and components and discuss some tips on how to write appropriate and effective professional letters. Examples of employment letters and routine business letters will also be provided.

Objectives

After completing this unit, you will be able to
◆ Identify different types of business letter formats;
◆ Understand the basic qualities that contribute to a good business letter;
◆ Edit writing for content, format, grammar and spelling;
◆ Produce professional quality business letters.

I Pre-class activities

Research and Explore

Task 1. Identify a job you may like to have in the future. Research the types of letters people in this job need to write. Find out the principles for writing business letters in this industry.

_____
_____
_____

Choose a piece of business writing that attracts your interest. What made you want to read it? Share your thoughts with your classmates.

___

___

___

Case study

Task 2. Both Sarah Jones and Lin Feng need to write follow-up letters after the job interview to show their good manners and make a good impression. Imagine you are Sarah Jones or Lin Feng. Discuss in groups how to plan and organize follow-up letters for the following situations. Take these factors into consideration:

(1) Sarah Jones hasn't got any response from the company two weeks after the job interview. She wants to send a letter to check on the status of the application and remind the recruiter that she is still interested in the job.

| Subject / Topic: |
| Purpose: |
| Recipient: |
| Key points to include: |
| Organization plan / Approach: |
| Style and tone: |

(2) Lin Feng has been invited for a second interview, which means being closer to the position. He is going to send a follow-up letter to leave his interviewer with a good impression and to demonstrate his interest, professionalism and suitability for the job.

Draft a follow-up letter based on one of the situations above.

☞ See the sample follow-up letter in Section Ⅲ.

 II   Introduction

Professional letters are formal documents sent externally to people like customers, clients, investors, suppliers, and government officials. Some business letters are sent internally, most often to employees or members within an organization. Personal business letters are written by individuals to deal with business matters. A job application letter, a customer complaint letter and a letter congratulating a business partner are examples of personal business letters. We use professional letters when we need to build goodwill, deliver bad news or discuss sensitive topics, exchange business information, and maintain a written record of formal communication. Professional letters should be clear, direct, courteous, and businesslike. They are often printed on letterhead paper and represent the business or organization.

Professional letter format

When writing a professional letter, select one of the common formats as shown in the example formats below.

Full Block Format 完全齐头式

No lines are indented.
All letter parts begin at the left margin.
The entire letter is left justified.
It is the most formal and popular style.

Semi-Block Format (Indented) 半齐头式

The writer's address, date, complimentary close, and signature are aligned to the right. Each paragraph is indented.
It is less formal than full block format.

Modified Block Format 改良齐头式

The writer's address, date, complimentary close, and signature are aligned to the right.
The body of the letter and the recipient's addresses are left justified.
It is less formal than full block format.

Parts of a Professional Letter

The essential parts of a professional letter:

letterhead, date, inside address, salutation, body of the letter, complimentary close, signature

The optional parts of a professional letter:

reference number, subject, enclosure, cC, postscript

(1) Letterhead / Return Address 信头

Most professional business correspondence is printed on a letterhead template. A letterhead contains the organization name, postal address, E-mail address, Web-site address, Telephone Number, Fax Number, Trade Mark or logo of the business (if any). It is usually printed on the top of the paper. Don't write your address if you use paper with a ready-printed letter head. If there is not such a letterhead, you may include a header with your address.

Exhibitions International	Exhibitions International
33, Kadoorie Avenue, Kowloon	33, Kadoorie Avenue, Kowloon
Phone: 9876 5432 E-mail: enquiries@xint.com.hk	Phone: 9876 5432
	E-mail: enquiries@xint.com.hk

(2) Date 日期

The month is spelled in full. The day is written in figures.

British English; day-month-year; American English:month-day-year

Exhibitions International 33, Kadoorie Avenue, Kowloon Phone: 9876 5432 E-mail: enquiries@xint.com.hk 10 October, 2013	**Acme Moving & Storage** 24 Regan Street Rochdale Lancashire LK 12 6DW 10 October, 2013

(3) Inside Address 信内地址

It begins one line below the date. This is the address of the recipient. It should include the person's full name, title (such as Ms., Mrs., Mr., or Dr.), full address, including city, state, and zip code.

It should be left justified, no matter which format you are using.

To a specific recipient	
Name ----------------------	Mr. Brian Palmer
Title ----------------------	Marketing Manager
Organization ------------	National Cooperative Publications
Street Address ----------	2499 Commerce Park Drive
City, State, zip code -----	Cleveland, Ohio 47239

To a department or an organization
  Below the address, write "**Attention**" (经办人) followed by your primary contact in that department.
  e.g. Attention: Human Resources Manager
      Attn: Public Relations Manager
      For the attention of Senior Administrative Officer
	Concorde International Corporation
	1746 Littlewoods Communications
	Woodsville, Massachusetts 01784
	
	Attention: Purchasing Manager

(4) Reference number 参考编号 / 案号

It is the file number of the business letter placed before the salutation. It is useful to refer to the previous letters which are related to the current letter. A reference line can refer to your files and / or your reader's files that have already been sent. You can use " Ref " as an abbreviation for "reference".

> Our reference: Project #239
> Your reference: Invoice #3444
> Ref: Your letter of Dec 22, 2010, file #1233445

(5) Subject / Re 标题 / 事由

A subject line is not necessary in a business letter. It is equivalent to Subject line in emails that helps the reader know the content of the message before reading. There are three common methods to distinguish the subject line from the body of the letter: place it right above or below salutation using "Subject" or "RE", type the subject in bold letters or type the subject in capital letters. The word subject is optional.

Subject: Loan Information Requested Dear Mr. Bowman: You are eligible to take out a loan from your company retirement account.　　　　　(American English)	Dear Mr. Fisher, **RE: Open job position for Arts consultant** I am interested in applying for the above-mentioned opening.　　　　　(British English)

(6) Salutation 称呼

The greetings like "Hi" "Hello guys" should only be used with people you are close to. Avoid using them in business letters.

You can use either mixed punctuation or open punctuation for the salutation and complimentary close. Mixed punctuation means putting a colon(:) after the salutation and a comma after the complementary close. Open punctuation means no punctuation follows salutation or complimentary close.

Very formal		**Less formal but still professional**	
To a named male or female	Dear Mr. Smith:　Dear Ms. Smith:	To a group of people	Dear colleagues
To a named person with titles of rank or honor	Dear Dr. Smith: Dear Prof. Smith: Dear President Smith:	To a named female	Dear Mary
If you are unsure of the recipient's gender, type the whole name	Dear Xu Lin:	To a named male	Dear John
To a position without a named contact	Dear Sir: Dear Sir / Madam:　Gentlemen: Dear Hiring Manager: Dear Personnel Department:		

(7) Body of the letter 信文

It starts one line below the greeting and consists of three paragraphs: the opening paragraph, the content paragraph, and the closing paragraph. Format the body according the block, semi-block, or modified block style. Most businesses use full block style. The body of the letter is single spaced, with a double space between paragraphs.

Opening paragraph

The opening paragraph is typically used to state the main point of the letter. Begin with a friendly opening then a statement of the main point.

It should state the purpose of the letter	• We are writing to inform you that… • I recently heard about…and would like to… • I would be interested in… • I am pleased to inform / announce / confirm… • We regret to inform you that…
It may refer to a previous contact (e.g. phone conversation, meeting, previous mail correspondence)	• I am writing regarding your inquiry about… • Thank you for your letter of… • In reply to your request,…

Body paragraphs

They give details or background information related to the purpose of the letter.

Write clearly and concisely. Let your reader know exactly what you are trying to say. You may choose organizational devices to emphasize the key points, such as a bullet list, or simply number them. Specific, meaningful information needs to be clear, concise, and accurate. Sentences should not be too long.

Closing paragraph

Call for action	• Please give this matter to your immediate attention. • I'll call you next Thursday to discuss this matter.
Express appreciation to the reader	• Thank you for your assistance with this matter.
Refer to future contact with the reader	• I look forward to meeting with you on 21 June.
Offer help	• If you have any questions or comments, please let us know.
Restate the purpose	• I apologize once again for the delay in responding.

(8) Complimentary close 结尾敬语

Closing statements are normally placed one or two lines under the conclusion. It should be in accordance with the salutation. "Yours" "Best", or "Cheers" are not suitable for business letters.

Very formal		Less formal but still professional	
When your letter starts with "Dear + Name"	Yours sincerely, Sincerely yours, Sincerely,	When you have some knowledge of the person to whom you are writing	Cordially Best regards Warm regards Best wishes
When your letter starts with "Dear Sir / Madam" or "To Whom It May Concern"	Yours faithfully,		

(9) Signature block 签名

It is five lines after the close, consisting of signature of the writer, the typed name, or the writer's title or position. Print and sing your full name. Don't sign your first name only or your initials only.

Use "pp" (代签)when you are signing the letter on someone's behalf. It stands for "Per Procurationem" which means "by the agency" or "on behalf of ".

Tim Smith	**Joana Sparks**
Tim Smith	p.p. Tim Smith
Vice President	Vice President

(10) Enclosure notation (optional) 附件

It indicates what is included with the letter, such as brochures, reports, or related business documents. It is usually shortened as **Enc,** or **ENC,** or **Inc,** or **Encl**. or **Incl**.

Enclosures (2): brochure, price list
Enc:1 Invoice

(11) Carbon copy notation 副本抄送

CC stands for carbon copy. It is required when copies of the letter are also sent to persons apart of the addressee.

cc: Bill Davis, Manager, Future Enterprise

(12) Postscript (PS) 附言

It serves two purposes: ① to re-emphasize a key point；② to be informal and personal. It may be handwritten or typed.

P.S. Just return the enclosed card to see if you aren't pleased with the service you receive!
PS. Give my regards to the others who had a part in making the program such a success.

Types of business letters

There are a variety of types of professional letters, which communicate good news, bad news, neutral news, or persuasive messages in the workplace. Each of these letters is written by following a formal format of letter writing and is unique and important in their own way.

Employment letters (the letters between job-givers and job-seekers)

Cover Letter / Application Letter, Follow-up Letter, Job Offer Letter, Job Rejection Letter, Job Acceptance Letter, Inquiry Letter, Employee Reference Letter, Letter of Recommendation, etc.

Business letters (the letters between organizations or companies)

Inquiry letter / Request letter, Thank-You Letter, Apology Letter, Congratulation Letter,

Farewell Letter, Promotion Announcement Letter, Resignation and Retirement Letter, Acknowledgment Letter, Sales Letter, Order Letter, Complaint Letter, Claim Letter, Adjustment Letter, etc..

Good news / informative: complaints and claims; reservations; appointments; orders; requests for action; inquiries about goods, people, or services; good news about hiring, credit, claims, and other good news.

Guidelines

When you write a business letter, keep in mind the key principles of effective letter writing.

Keep it Strong
- Answer the reader's question in the first paragraph.
- Give your answer and then explain why.
- Use concrete words and examples.
- Keep to the subject. Keep it Sincere.
- Answer promptly.
- Be human and as friendly as possible.

Keep it Short
- Cut needless words and needless information.
- Cut stale phrases and redundant statements.
- Cut the first paragraph if it refers to previous correspondence.

Keep it Simple
- Use familiar words, short sentences and short paragraphs.
- Keep your subject matter as simple as possible.
- Keep related information together.
- Use a conversational style.

III Letter Examples

The following are different types of professional letters written in different formats. These letters are only furnished as business letter examples for instructional purposes only. They are not meant to be and should not be considered real letters. Use them as a guide to assist you in writing more effective business letters.

1. Inquiry letter in modified block style.

This is an interview follow-up letter where Sarah Jones politely enquires about the status of her job application and affirms her interest in the job. The letter is written in a friendly, courteous and professional tone.

写信人地址 日期		5555 Hemlock St Sacramento, CA 95841 July 8, 2012	Return address Date
收信人姓名 地址	Mr. John Smith Corefact Corporation 1000 Greenwood Ave Sacramento, CA 95821		Inside address
称呼	Dear Mr. Smith,		Salutation
礼貌客气地询问，重申对职位的兴趣	I hope all is well. I know how busy you probably are, but it has been two weeks since the interview and I look forward to hearing from you regarding the position of Office Manager. If the position is still open, I would like to again express my interest in working with you at Corefact.		Introduction: Purpose of letter
	During the interview, you have mentioned that you are looking for a hardworking and enterprising person to fill a position in your department. I am sure that I have what it takes and am still interested in the job.		Body: Details related to your message
展示积极态度，愿意提供相关信息	Perhaps it may be worthwhile to meet once again and explore the many ways in which I could benefit your company. If necessary, I would be glad to resend my resume or to provide any further information you might need regarding my candidacy. I can be reached at 555-555-5555 or jdoe@abcd.com. I look forward to hearing from you.		Closing: Request for action or goodwill comments
结尾敬语		Sincerely	Complementary close
手写签名 打印姓名		*Sarah Jones* Sarah Jones	Signature Printed name

2. Thank-you letter or goodwill letter in semi block style.

This follow-up letter is written to gain the advantage over the other job candidates and build goodwill with the employer by expressing sincere gratitude and specifying why he is the preferred job candidate.

Unit 5   Professional letters

日期	Date
信内地址	Name Address City, State Zip Code
称呼	Dear Ms. Maggi,
信文	I take this opportunity to thank you and your staff for the friendliness and warmth extended to me during my interview last week. I enjoyed every bit being there and I hope I will soon be on board to form an integral part of your organization.

(Direct approach)
Introduction:
Expresses gratitude and passion

I love facing challenges and your interview was one of such kind with the challenging aptitude tests, followed by the personal interview. I would like to stress that the interview had given me a very good insight of this profession. My skill set and knowledge would prove very helpful to take the firm to a new level.

Details: Demonstrates the understanding of the job and how it fits into the company

Apart from possessing the right qualifications and experience, I also possess very good communication skills, suitable for this profile of a Software Engineer. I am very devoted towards my work and can even give extra hours if needed be.

Highlights the attributes that make him the best candidate

For future evidence of my qualifications as a software engineer intern, I have enclosed two reference letters which confirm my skills and work ethic. If you have any doubts or need any clarifications, please feel free to call me at your convenience.

Closing:
Maintains goodwill and expresses appreciation

Again, thank you for your time and consideration. I look forward to a positive response from your end.

Sincerely yours,

Lin Feng

Lin Feng.
Enclosures: 2 Reference letters

结尾敬语

手写签名
打印姓名

附件

Enclosure notation with relevant description

3. Job offer letter for the paid intern in full block style (good news letter).

This is a formal business letter notifying the job candidate of a job offer and to document terms and conditions related to this position. It is a good news business letter serving as the legal basis for employment. The letter is formal, serious, professional, positive and welcoming.

115

3-4F, B22, 10 Jiu Xian Qiao Lu
Chao Yang District,
Beijing, 100015

May 18, 2018
Name
Address
City, State Zip Code

Re: Internship Offer
Dear Mr. Lin:

On behalf of Intel Company, I am pleased to extend to you this offer of temporary employment as an Intern, reporting to Mr. Bennett. If you accept this offer, you will begin your internship on June 1, 2018, and will be expected to work 5 days per week.

You will be paid 30 yuan per hour, less applicable taxes and withholdings. As a temporary employee, you will not receive any of the employee benefits that regular company employees receive, including, but not limited to, health insurance, vacation or sick pay, or paid holidays.

Your internship is expected to end on December 1, 2018. However, your internship with the company is "at-will," which means that either you or the company may terminate your internship at any time, with or without cause and with or without notice.

By accepting this offer, you agree that throughout your internship, you will observe all policies and practices governing the conduct of our business and employees. This letter sets forth the complete offer we are extending to you, and supersedes and replaces any prior inconsistent statements or discussions. It may be changed only by a subsequent written agreement.

If you accept this offer, please sign below and return it no later than close of business on May 20, 2018. If you have any questions, please contact me. I hope that your association with Intel will be successful and rewarding.

Sincerely yours,

Andrew Melvin

Andrew Melvin
Human Resources Manager

I accept employment with the Intel Company on the terms and conditions set out in this letter.

_____   _____
Signature   Date

4. Job acceptance letter.

This letter is written in response to the job offer letter above, and usually precedes the actual employment contract. The job candidate responds in a professional and polite manner to his job offer.

> Dear Mr. Melvin:
> Thank you for sending me your formal job offer so promptly. It is with great enthusiasm that I accept the position of Software Engineer Intern with Intel and look forward to starting employment with your company.
>
> I thoroughly reviewed the details of the position in the letter of employment I received. I understand that the internship begins on June 1, 2018. As we discussed, my starting salary will be 30 *yuan* per hour less applicable taxes and withholdings. As requested, I have signed it and promptly sent it back to you at the address listed above. As suggested I have kept the second copy.
>
> If you need any additional information or paperwork, please contact me at 138×××××××. I am eager to join your team and make a positive contribution to the company.
> Sincerely,
> *Lin Feng*
> Lin Feng

5. Termination of agreement letter (bad news letter).

This is a bad news letter notifying the customer of the termination of their service agreement. The writer tries to maintain a good relationship with the client while breaking the bad news. The letter is courteous and straightforward.

Letter	Annotations
June 29, 2017 Dear Mr. Kirk: Our records indicate that over the past year, we have received frequent calls from you regarding your billing or other general account information. While we have worked to resolve your issues and questions to the best of our ability, the number of inquiries you have made to us during this time has led us to determine that we are unable to meet your current wireless needs.	(Indirect approach) Introduction: Offers background and reasons showing that the decision is fair and reasonable. Avoids blaming the customer
Therefore, after careful consideration, the decision has been made to terminate your wireless service agreement effective July 30, 2017. This will allow you to pursue and engage with another wireless carrier.	Body: States the bad news clearly and politely, showing You-attitude
We understand that having to switch to another wireless carrier may be an inconvenience, and we want to do everything possible to help you during this transition. So, a credit has been applied to your account to bring your current balance to zero. In addition, we will not require you to pay an Early Termination Fee and you are free to transfer your number to another carrier. You will, however, need to initiate the transfer of your number with the carrier of your choice before July 30, 2017 as the number will no longer be available as of that date.	Offers further assistance to minimize the trouble to the customer
Should you have any questions regarding the transfer of your number to another wireless carrier or about the final adjustments to your account, please call our customer care department at (877)527-8405. Sincerely Sprint Nextel Corporation	Closing: Ends with positive statements to promote goodwill

IV Writing skills

Organizing information strategically

When organizing professional letters, you need to consider how the audience will understand and accept the information. The proper placement of information will make the reader more receptive to your information.

Information in the first paragraph of a letter or the first and last sentence of a paragraph tends to be read and remembered better. Information buried in the middle of a paragraph or a letter is easily overlooked or forgotten. Therefore, you can emphasize or de-emphasize the information by placing it in different areas of a letter depending on the audience reaction and the message type.

When you anticipate no resistance to the message, you can use the direct approach by putting the main point of the message or important information at the beginning of a letter. Whenever possible, use the direct approach because most readers want the main point front.

If you have some difficult things to say or bad news to deliver, you need to adopt the indirect approach. You can reveal the bad news in the body of the message, a supporting sentence or a subordinate clause so as to soften the blow. Although the indirect approach has its advantages, some readers may still prefer the direct statement of bad news instead of a lengthy letter revealing the bad news in the middle. Therefore, consider the specific audience and length of your letter before choosing the direct or indirect approach.

If you decide to send out unsolicited sales letters, you need to ensure that each recipient becomes interested in reading your letter. The AIDA model can help you to write in a way that catches the reader's interest right away.

The following table shows the relationship between message type, audience reaction and the approach for organizing information.

Message type	Audience reaction	Organizational approach
Good news, neutral message, or good will	Neutral, interested, or pleased	Direct approach (1) Main idea / Purpose (2) Explanation / Details (3) Polite closing or call to action
Bad news or rejection	Disappointed, angry, frustrated, or resistant	Indirect approach (1) Buffer (appreciation / positive opening) (2) Explanation / Alternative (3) Bad news (4) Positive, forward-looking closing

Message type	Audience reaction	Organizational approach
Persuasive news (that needs to convince the reader), sales	Uninterested or unwilling	AIDA approach (1) Attention: A statement or question that captures attention. (2) Interest: Arouse the audience's interest in the subject. (3) Desire: Build the audience's desire to comply. (4) Action: Request action or build goodwill.

Task 3. Put the sentences in the correct order to form business letters. Consider what organizational pattern should be appropriate for the message and how to arrange information.

Message 1

(1) I wish you and the committee great success in achieving this year's goal.

(2) This year I am involved in developing a new department here at the clinic that is taking up all my time. While I would enjoy working with BCCJ again, I am afraid that I wouldn't be able to give the duties the attention the project deserves.

(3) Your invitation for me to act as chairperson for BCCJ's upcoming Annual Auction Dinner is an honor. I enjoyed serving in that role last year.

(4) Perhaps I may suggest one of my colleagues who would have the time to do the job the way it ought to be done. Give me a call if you are interested, and I will be happy to suggest some names for you.

Message 2

(1) I have known Mr. John for more than five years, being his Professor of Macroeconomics at National Goodwell University.

(2) Being a witness to his motivation and passion for learning, I am sure that Mr. John will continue to be at the top of his class and continue to display exceptional academic performance in whichever college he gets into.

(3) It is with much pleasure and enthusiasm that I am writing this letter of recommendation for Mr. John.

(4) Mr. John is an exceptional student with amazing academic ability. He presents extraordinary logical thinking abilities and an intellectual curiosity which is distinctive from his peers. He was always an active participant in classes who listened eagerly and never hesitated to raise questions.

Establishing the right style and tone

To communicate effectively and project a positive image, you should adjust the style and tone for your professional letter according to the recipient and purpose. It is essential that you know when to be formal, conversational, firm, friendly, or apologetic depending on situation and your purpose.

1. Write in a professional and conversational style.

Unlike personal letters, most business letters are written in a formal style for official purposes. When you represent yourself or your company to show your respect, build the credibility and trustworthiness of business, you should keep your writing at a professional level. A professional style usually requires complex sentences, sophisticated vocabulary, and standard grammar and spelling.

However, formal does not mean stuffy and pretentious. A business letter will sound unnatural if it is filled with unnecessarily long sentences, obscure words, jargons, and cliches. Modern business letter style uses more short sentences, active voice, everyday, concrete, and precise words. This style works well with external readers and others you are not acquainted with. So, for most situations in the workplace, you can write the way you talk, i.e., write in a professionally conversational style, and avoid texting language and slang.

e.g.

I acknowledge receipt of your letter and I beg to thank you. (too formal, unnatural)

Thank you for your letter. (conversational, natural)

Thans for your letter. (casual)

Task 4. Compare each pair of sentences and discuss which sentence is overly formal or pretentious for most business letters.

(1) a. Please apprise me of what transpired at the meeting.

　　b. Please tell me what happened at the meeting.

(2) a. Our team leader deems it imperative that we conduct ourselves ethically.

　　b. Our team leader insists that we conduct ourselves ethically.

(3) a. Herewith we are returning a brochure that describes our health care exchange.

　　b. We are returning a brochure that describes our health care exchange.

(4) a. The undersigned hereby acknowledges the receipt of your letter.

　　b. I have received your letter.

2. Adopt You-attitude.

• **Focus on the recipient's needs, purposes, or interests instead of your own.**

Avoid a self-centered attitude focusing on your own concerns rather than those of the recipient. Try to empathize with your readers. Ask yourself: what do they want, what do they need to know, and what's in it for them?

When you are writing goodwill letters or routine letters, don't make your message all about "me" or "us". Using the second person (you, your, and yours) can help establish a good relationship with your reader.

When making requests or suggestions, it might be a better choice to use the following phrases to sound less direct and more polite:

e.g.

"I was hoping…" "Would you be able to…?" "Do you think you might be able to…?" "I was thinking we could…" "You might want to think about…" "It might be a good idea…"

(Indirect and polite)

If you're trying to persuade your readers to buy a product, accept an offer, pay a bill, or perform a service for you, emphasize what your reader will benefit from it.

e.g.

We are happy to announce that transaction can be made even after 3:00 PM till 5:00 PM at the teller-counter. **(Me-attitude)**

You will be able to do transactions after office hours at the Teller counter till 5:00 PM.

(You-attitude)

• Find the positive ways to deliver bad news or criticize.

When you have to deliver bad news, you must watch your tone. Be tactful and diplomatic. If you sound impolite, impatient, angry or frustrated, your reader will not respond to solve your problem quickly. To convey bad news tactfully, you can:

• <u>Avoid negatives</u> words such as "cannot" "never" "forbid" "fail" "impossible" "refuse" "prohibit" "restrict", and "deny" as much as possible.

• <u>Use the passive voice</u> to avoid blaming the reader for the problem.

• <u>Put the negative message in a subordinate</u> clause such as "Although…, we…" and "Because…, it is…" to soften the tone or introduce an alternative solution.

• <u>Give specific reasons or explanations</u> to make the bad news easier to accept.

• <u>Include good news, appreciation or recognition statement, compliment, objective facts or apology</u> as the buffer.

• <u>Use objective, non-judgmental, and nondiscriminatory language</u>.

e.g.

(1) You have failed to send us the credit card.

(We-attitude, Use active voice; critical, unfriendly)

The credit card has not been sent to us.

(You-attitude, Use passive voice; objective, tactful)

(2) I think your computers suck and I am never buying them again.

(We-attitude, Use negative language; impolite, emotional)

I am disappointed with the quality of computers purchased from your company, and I plan to take my business elsewhere in the future.

(You-attitude. Use objective language; polite, objective)

(3) We do not allow smoking in the main building. **(We-attitude. Harsh, cold)**

(4) Although smoking is not allowed in the main building, we have set aside 3 outdoor smoking areas. **(You-attitude. Use a subordinate clause; polite)**

We are sorry to inform you that your suggestions on how to use the left-over budget money have been rejected. **(We-attitude. Unfriendly)**

Thank you for your great suggestions on how to use the left-over budget money. Unfortunately, we are not able to get your ideas approved because we have already allocated the money to the local library. **(You-attitude. Include appreciation and explanations)**

Task 5. Improve the following sentences to convey more positive attitudes.

(1) I reviewed your suggestion that we hire an additional secretary. I am not going to consider new staff at this time.

_____

(Hint: Thank you for…I…and agree that…Unfortunately, I would not…because… / Perhaps we could…)

(2) If you do not complete and return this enclosed advertisement contract by July 1, 19××, we will sell you your advertisement space to some other clients.

_____

(Hint: Please… so that you can… / After this deadline, we will…)

(3) Because of the amount of information you request in your letter, I simply cannot help you without seriously disrupting my work schedule.

_____

(Hint: In your letter you request…which I would like to… Because of…, however, I will be able to answer only….)

(4) While I am willing to discuss changes in specific aspects of this article or ideas on additional areas to cover, I am not prepared to change the basic theme of the article.

_____

(Hint: I am open to…about…However, I do want to retain…)

V Exercises and Practice

Writing the date, salutation, and complimentary close

Task 6. Based on the information given below, put the date, salutation, and complimentary close in the right position of a letter. Identify the type of the letter format.

Unit 5 Professional letters

(1) Suppose you are Jane Brown, the Purchasing Manager of Fine Foods Ltd. You are writing a letter to Reed Jones with Thames Software Systems to inquire about Stock Control Software System. The date is 12th of September, 2006.

(2) Suppose you are Robert Hibbing, General Manager of KR Toys. You are writing a letter to the Marketing Director of a company to introduce your business. You don't know the recipient's name and gender.

```
                              Fine Foods Ltd.
                              10 Bridge Street
                              London
                              SW10 5TG
Reed. Jones
Sales Manager
Thames Software Systems
River Buildings
Stockwell Walk
London
SW17 5HG

_____
_____
_____
```

```
                              KR Toys
                              3444 Elm Drive
                              Wichita, KS 66500

Marketing Director
6999 Main Street
Chicago, IL 88998

_____
_____
_____
_____
```

Writing the opening paragraph

Task 7. Complete the following opening sentences with the appropriate words.

(1) This letter is to bring to your _____ a problem I had with the cellphone I purchased from your store on July 12, 2015. **(Complain)**

(2) This letter is _____ your complaint letter _____ the defective product that you purchased from our store. I sincerely _____ on behalf of FUY Inc. for the inconvenience this has _____ you. **(Apologize / Respond to a complaint)**

(3) Please accept my sincere _____ on your promotion to regional manager. You are definitely the right person for the job. **(Congratulate)**

(4) I am currently in my last year of high school and am exploring the various possibilities for further studies. I would, therefore, like to _____ more about your college programs, as well as the necessary steps for the admissions process. **(Inquire)**

(5) With _____ to your advertisement in yesterday's New York Times, I would like to request a copy of your latest edition of catalog. **(Request)**

(6) Thank you for your _____ of 12 September asking for the latest edition of our catalog. As you can see from the _____ brochure, we would like to _____ you that it is possible to make purchases online at jacksonbros.com. **(Respond to a request)**

(7) _____ our final meeting last Wednesday, on behalf of my company, I am _____ to offer your company the contract for the Bremner Shopping Mall. **(Deliver good news)**

(8) I would like to sincerely_____ for accepting the partnership with our organization; ABC International. We_____ you that this venture between TechSmart Pvt Ltd. and ABC International will benefit both the organizations for a very long period. **(Thank)**

Task 8. Translate the following opening sentences into English.

(1) 高兴地通知您，您的项目建议书已经获得审批，我们想约您当面签署协议。
_____
_____

(2) 我正在应聘销售部经理一职，如能提供介绍信，不胜感激。
_____
_____

(3) 我谨代表组委会邀请您参加即将到来的"2017 年国际残疾儿童研究会议"，并请您担任主旨发言人和嘉宾。
_____
_____

(4) 兹函复贵公司五月二十日的询问，随函附上最新的商品目录。
_____
_____

(5) 现就我 9 月 10 日的那封信作进一步说明，我方可以确定，你们所要的零件都有现货。
_____
_____

Writing the concluding paragraph

Task 9. Read the messages below and write closing remarks for each situation. Consider the following ways to end a message: call to action, express appreciation, offer help, develop goodwill, refer to future contact, restate the purpose, etc. *(e.g. I look forward to …; Please…if…; Thank you for …; I wish you…)*

(1) A letter to the organizer of the seminar confirming attendance and talk on a seminar. (Response letter, good news)

Unit 5　Professional letters

Dear Ms. Shenaz Nalwala:

I am pleased to be considered and invited to be a part of this great experience and would like to confirm that I will be attending the marketing seminar as the guest of honor. I am so excited and happy to share my knowledge with the students of N.M University.

As per the information that I have received, the seminar is to be held on the 27 January, 2015 from 8 a.m. onwards. I am well aware of the topics that you had to send, enclosed with the invitation letter and I have reviewed them well. I make sure that the students will have a well informed and knowledgeable seminar.

_____

(2) A letter to a publishing house requesting the permission to use copyrighted material. (Request letter, neutral news)

Dear Sir:

I write this letter to bring to your knowledge that I am completing a doctoral thesis on the biothermal energy studies at J.H.B. College. Since Dr. Eastwind Cooper is renowned in the area of biothermal energy studies, I request you to kindly grant me permission to quote extensive parts of his book 'Quantitative Analysis of Biothermal Energy on Mars as Defined By NASA' in the thesis. The author's name and publication details will be duly mentioned in the footnotes and the bibliography. I assure you that the information will not be used otherwise except for the sole purpose mentioned.

_____ I am enclosing a duplicate copy of this letter for your records.

(3) A letter to an employee informing him that he has been laid off. (Layoff letter, bad news)

Dear Abigail:

As you already know, the company has been struggling with the rising costs of production and the falling prices caused by the overseas competition. Unfortunately, your post is being eliminated, since we had no other go on this matter, effective October 15. This layoff is not related to individual performance and we encourage you to express your opinion about the same.

The payment that is due will be reached to you on or before the last day of your working with this company. The insurance company will contact you for letting you know about their procedures on this matter.

You have been a valuable member of our team, and we deeply regret the economic downturn that has made this workforce reduction necessary. _____

(4) A letter thanking your customer for referring another individual to your company.(Thank-you letter, good news)

Dear Mr. Max,

I would deeply like to thank you from the bottom of my heart for suggesting Mr. Kent to our "Quick Delivery" services. It was a great pleasure to have him at our shop. Your faith in us has made us work even more expertly to stand up to your expectations.

Mr. Kent was satisfied with our customer service experience and has placed a bulk order with us for delivery at his house. All this happened only because of your recommendation.

Putting it all together

Task 10. Put the following words and phrases in the blanks.

A. Thank you for choosing	B. Unfortunately	C. We're delighted to	D. request
E. This letter confirms	F. We sincerely apologize for	G. We would appreciate	H. We decide to
I. hope for your consideration	J. If you wish to contact us regarding this reservation		

(1) Hotel reservation letter / Request letter

Dear Reservation Department:

Greeting from Amir LCC.

_____ reserve a room with one king-size bed for two adults for three nights, from March 24 through March 26, 2015 at the corporate rate. We will be attending the Springfield History Association's annual convention, 2015.

_____ receiving a written confirmation before March 1.

Sincerely,
Henry Marzetti
Amir LCC

(2) Reply letter confirming hotel reservation / Confirmation letter

Dear Mr Marzetti,

_____ the Springfield Hotel. _____ have you as our guest and hope you will enjoy everything our hotel and local area and attractions have to offer.

_____ your request for one room for a stay of three nights, from

March 24 through March 26, 2015. The rate is 258 € per night. We have made your reservations at the Springfield Hotel. The total charge to your credit card is 810 €, including taxes. Cancellations will not be accepted after March 23.

_____, please refer to confirmation #123456.

Sincerely,

Rod Connor
Reservation Manager
the Springfield Hotel

(3) Cancellation of reservation letter / Apology letter / Bad news letter

Dear Mr. Connor:

We reserved the room at your hotel for the Springfield History Association's annual convention on March 19. _____, since we recently had a reorganization, we need to cancel our reservation and respectfully _____ a reimbursement of our deposit.

_____ any inconvenience on your part. When everything is already settled, we hope to transact with you again.

Thank you for your kind service and _____.

Sincerely,

Henry Marzetti
Amir LCC

Formality of language

Task 11. A list of formal words are given in the box below. Read the sentences taken from different letters and replace the underlined words with their formal equivalents. Change the form of the word if necessary.

convenient	concerning	numerous	review	ensure	angry
at your earliest convenience		enquire	inform	assure	
supply	delighted	request	terminate	furthermore	

(1) I am <u>happy</u> to inform you that you have been selected to be our new sergeant. _____

(2) Please confirm if this date and time is <u>OK</u> for you. _____

(3) Please <u>go over</u> the proposal and make any necessary changes. _____

(4) I am writing <u>about</u> the current situation with the Skipton Airport Project. _____

(5) We have <u>a lot of</u> questions which we hope you could answer. _____

(6) I can promise you this will never happen again. _____

(7) We will make sure the computer is repaired by one of our technicians. _____

(8) He's really mad about the service he received at our store. _____

(9) She asked for a copy of the latest project report yesterday. _____

(10) We regret to tell you that we shall have to end the contract. _____

(11) I am writing to ask about the possibility of an internship position in Seattle. _____

(12) Any information you give will be treated confidentially. _____

(13) Please sort it out ASAP. _____

(14) I work a full-time job during the day, plus I go to school at night. _____

Task 12. The right-hand column shows the less formal phrases for writing letters or emails. Supply the more formal equivalent for each phrase in the left-hand column.

Purpose		More formal	Less formal
Request	(1)	_____	Could you…?
Inquire	(2)	_____	I want to ask if…
Notify	(3)	_____	Just want to let you know…
Apologize	(4)	_____	Sorry for the delay in replying.
	(5)	_____	Sorry for the inconvenience.
	(6)	_____	I / We are very sorry…
Give good ews	(7)	_____	I am / will be happy to…
Give bad news	(8)	_____	I am sorry to have to tell you that…
	(9)	_____	Sorry, I'm afraid I can't…
Thank	(10)	_____	Thank you for your...
Complain	(11)	_____	I wanted to inform you about…
	(12)	_____	I'd like to complain about…
	(13)	_____	I'm very dissatisfied with…
Closing remarks	(14)	_____	Ring me at…
	(15)	_____	Hope to hear from you soon.
	(16)	_____	You can call me if you need anything.

Unit 5 Professional letters

Task 13. Rewrite this message using a more formal style. Use the appropriate phrases from previous exercises.

Hi Bruce,

Just want to let you know that I must cancel the meeting for Tuesday, January 18th at 10 a.m. . Something unexpected has arisen and I have to cancel our appointment. But I still want to meet with you, and would like to schedule another appointment. Is Tuesday, January 25th at 11 a.m. OK with you? Please ring me or email me to let me know.

Sorry again for any inconvenience this may cause. Hope to see you soon.

Regards,

Mandy

Editing and proofreading

Task 14. Identify the weaknesses or errors in the following letter. Correct the errors and revise the letter so that it is clearer, easier to read, and more professional. Here are the changes you should make:

(1) wrong placement of the main idea (the bad news); (2) lacks you-attitude; (3) informal expressions in opening line and closing; (4) one or more typos; (5) a fragment; (6) incorrect layout of letter; (7) wrong word in subject line.

123 Winner's Road New Employee Town, PA 54321 Ernie James 1234 Writing Lab Lane White City, IN 12345 RE: Travel request deny Dear Mr James: I'm sorry to tell you that your request for travel funds to travel to the Syllabus Conference in Santa Clara, California, has been denied. The university has limited funds available for travel this year and although I know you really want to go, I can't afford to give you the $1 500 you requested (which by the way is a lot too requst at this late date at the current time of this request). I hope you understand our position because we really want our faculty to be happy. Even though I can't pay for this trip, I encourage you to apply again for future travel money. Because I hope to receive more money budgeted for travel the next fiscal year of 2014/2015. Thank you again for your request. I always strive to help faculty fund their travels. Yours Tracy J. Hall March 16, 2013	Revision

Assignments

1. Compose professional letters.

Work in pairs. Student A chooses Task A for each situation and complete a full standard business letter. Section B chooses Task B to respond to the letter in Task A.

(1) **A: Inquiry letter / Request letter.** You are Jack Jetis, the Managing Director of Golden Gate Engineering. You saw a training course on Quality Control from the advert of a corporation in the HK Daily. Write a letter to ProSkills Training Centre, Jubilee Building, Silver Road, Wan Chai 560022, asking if they would offer a 7-day training course on Quality Control for 20

managers. You need their answers to your questions about the teaching staff and the possible schedule for the course. Please write in full block style.

B: Reply to the inquiry. Imagine you are Mary Palmer. Write a reply to Jack Jetic on behalf of ProSkills Training Centre and enclose a brochure that will provide answers to the questions. Jack Jetic's mailing address is Golden Gate Engineering Inc., 345, Nathan Rd, Prince Square, Kowloon, H.K. Please write in semi-block style.

(2) **A: Complaint Letter.** You are David Crampton, one of the managers who attended the training coursed offered by ProSkills Training Centre August 10-17, 2010. Write a complaint letter to Emily Eastwood, the Head Trainor of ProSkills Training Centre. Explain that you were dissatisfied with the speakers because they started arriving late and cut short the sessions in the second half of the course. You ask for the refund of training fees.

B: Reply to the complaint letter. You are Emily Eastwood, the Head Trainor of ProSkills Training Centre. Respond to the claim letter in Task A. Respond to David Crampton's cliam letter, informing him that his claim has been examined and verified, and you promise to settle his claim. Request him to reply this letter as acceptance of the claim adjustment.

2. Check and evaluate professional letters.

Use the following checklist to revise and polish the final draft of your letter for Task A. Exchange your letter with your partner. Evaluate your partner's letter, pointing out its strengths and weaknesses.

Professional letter checklist

Organization	Appearance
• Includes the essential parts: heading, salutation, introduction, body, closure, and signature • Arranges information appropriately (direct or indirect approach)	• Uses correct business letter format: full block, semi-block or modified semi-block • Uses spacing and fonts appropriately
Content • Introduction: Letter clearly states the purpose or the main point • Body: Gives enough details and facts to support the main point • Conclusion: Restates the reasons or • Easy to follow	**Language** • Tone is appropriate for intended reader • Accurate use of punctuation and grammar • No spelling errors
Comments Anything that could be improved? Anything that you particularly like?	

Unit 6 Professional Emails

> E-mail has become the dominant form of communication in the workplace because of its convenience, efficiency and low cost. Being able to write a polished, professional email is now a critical skill both in college and the workplace. Effective professional email writing requires professionalism, efficiency, politeness and brevity. This unit will teach you how to harness the power of a truly effective professional email. You will look at different email formats and examples to analyze formality level, tone, and various organizational styles.

Objectives

After completing this unit, you will be able to
◆ Identify the main parts of an email message;
◆ Understand the principles of effective business emails;
◆ Write effective subject lines;
◆ Design email messages for easy reading;
◆ Use appropriate email styles and tone for your audience;
◆ Produce professional quality business emails.

 I   Pre-class activities

📎Research and Explore

Task 1. Do preliminary reading and research on the following questions and get prepared for class discussion.
(1) What are the business email etiquette rules you need to know?

_____
_____
_____

(2) Work in pairs or groups and present a set of rules for writing business emails based on the Case Study below.

🔊 Case study

Task 2. Lin Feng has received an email from IT Department announcing a staff meeting. This email message is grammatical and free of errors in spelling and mechanics. However, he still finds it difficult to read and skim. Read and evaluate the email message and discuss the following questions:

(1) What are weaknesses of this email? What makes the message difficult to read and understand?

(2) Does this email communicate ideas clearly and effectively? Does it present too much information or unnecessary information?

(3) Do you think the style and tone is appropriate for email? Underline the expressions or structures that you think are too formal for this email.

Try rewriting this email so that it is brief and has the right level of formality for an email. Compare your revision with the sample email given in Section III.

(Original version)

> Dear all:
>
> Please be advised that we will be holding our regular monthly meeting at which your attendance as a member of the team is requested. The meeting will be held at 4 p.m. on Thursday, March 12, in the small conference room. The agenda of the meeting is to discuss work completed, upcoming milestones, project risks, and open issues. We have noticed that not all members of the department have been attending such meetings due to the pressure of work; thus, we are sending this notice to remind you of the meeting so that you can rearrange your schedule in advance. In line with this, concerned staff members are requested to give an update on our current projects prior to the meeting.
>
> If you are unable to attend this meeting for any reason, it will be appreciated if you notify Mary at extension 5555 by noon the day of the meeting.
>
> Stephen King

☞ See Section IV for help.

Task 3. Lin Feng needs to complete his project progress report before the monthly meeting. He emails his project team leader to ask for a favor. The email, however, sounds impolite and casual, which is not appropriate when writing to someone in authority. Circle the words or phrases that are too informal or too direct.

> Hey Jack!
>   How are you? I'm working on my project progress report. Could you review it before I submit? I need your comments and suggestions cos it is the first project report I've written. I'll send you the draft report in two days, so please keep checking your inbox. Thanks!!
> Write soon.
> See ya!
> Lin Feng

II Introduction

Organizations use email for informal and formal, internal and external communications. E-mail messages range from being short and direct to chatty and conversational. Formal emails are similar to letters. Formal emails are usually sent to people the writer doesn't know or to people outside the company. Semi-formal emails are usually sent to people the writer doesn't know very well. Informal emails are sent between colleagues. If you are not sure how formal your email should be, copy the email style of the person who wrote to you, or use a semi-formal style. It is very important to remember, however, that issues of clarity and correctness are just as important in formal email messages as they are in printed materials.

Parts of an email

E-mail header

From	The address of the sender. Use a professional email address
To	The address of the recipient(s) Recipients in the To field are expected to reply or follow up to the email.
Cc	carbon copy / courtesy copy = Cc The address of other recipients, which will be shown to all. The recipients in the Cc field are usually the sender's supervisors, but they do not need to reply the email.
Bcc	blind courtesy copy = Bcc The address of the recipient(s), which will not be shown to other recipients. Use the BCC field cautiously.

From	Ramsey, Tim <TRamsey@gamil.com>
To	Marietta Brown
Cc	Michael Sun
Bcc	
Subject	RE: Please forward this to librarian.

Subject Line

The subject lines summarize the message and provide the reason the message is being sent.

It is short, usually a word or a phrase.	• *Arrival Date of Order 395*
It should not be too general.(e.g. *Hello, Reply, Meeting, etc.*)	• *Application for a License*
	• *Congratulations on Passing your Exams*
It should be more specific.	• *Proposal for Waste Reduction*
Do not put a full stop at the end of subject headings.	• *In voice 2390 Attached*

Salutation

Salutations or greetings can be formal or informal, depending on the situation. A salutation can be followed by a colon(:) or a comma(,). A colon is often considered more formal in some countries, although more people prefer to use a comma after the salutation and closing greeting.

Formal emails

writing to someone when you don't know by name	*Dear Sir or Madam Dear Sir / Madam*
writing to someone when you know the name	*Dear Mr. Thomas Dear Dr. Thomas* *Dear Ms Thomas Dear John Thomas*
writing to a group	*Dear all To my clients: To: All sales staff*

Semi-formal emails

writing to someone when you know the name	*Dear John Dear Olivia*

Informal emails

writing to your colleagues (In most organization, people address each other by their first names in emails)	*Hi John Hello Olivia John Olivia* *Hi Hello Hey*
writing to a group	*Hi everyone Hi, team*

Message

Limit the content to one screen, if possible. Write proper paragraphs and leave spaces between paragraphs. A paragraph is often two or three sentences long and only contains a single point. When you start writing about a new topic, you can start a new paragraph.

(1) Opening paragraph: provides the topic and the purpose of your message.

(2) Body paragraphs: provide the necessary background and details.

(3) Ending paragraph: brings the message to a close or provides a specific call for needed action.

Opening paragraph

When responding to an email or inquiry If there has been some kind of recent previous contact	• Thanks for your email about… / enquiry about… / for meeting me… / for your phone call / for the information about… / inviting me… **(Formal)** *Thank you for your interest in our…* *Thank you for your prompt response.* • In reply to your email, … • As requested, here is… • After having received your…, I …
If there hasn't been any recent contact	• Sorry it has taken me so long to write back. • Sorry for my late reply.
When initiating an email or inquiry **Giving the purpose** If there hasn't been any recent contact	• I'm writing to you about / concerning / with regard to/in connection with / regarding… • I am writing to enquire about/inform you of / ask / check / clarify / confirm / reserve / book / suggest / arrange… **(Formal)** • I'm writing to let you know… / request /tell you / thank you… / ask for further details about… / inform you that my new address is… / complain about your customer service. / say thank you very much for all your hard work. • Just a short email / quick note to say… **(Less formal)** • Just a few comments about…
If you write to someone for the first time	• I am…, the director of … Company. I saw your advertisement in… • I was given your contact details by… • …said I should write to you about…
If you write to people who you don't know well	• I hope you are well. **(Less formal)**
If you write to people you know well (colleagues and long-term clients)	• How are you? / How's it going? / How are things? / How's life? • How was your holiday in Hawaii? • Hope you had a good weekend. **(Less formal)**

Closing paragraph

Show goodwill	• Thank you for your time and I look forward to hearing back from you. **(Formal)** • Thank you for your cooperation / assistance with… • Have a nice day / weekend **(Less formal)**

(Continued)

Focus on a future action	• We look forward to / I'm looking forward to your reply / hearing from you (Formal) • We look forward to a successful working relationship in the future / your continued participation / support / assistance on this matter • Looking forward to seeing you / your response on this matter (Less formal) • I hope to see you again soon. • See you then. • I'll check and get back to you. • Please let me know if that's okay. • I'll speak to you when I get back.
Offer help	• If I could be of any assistance, do not hesitate to let me know. (Formal) • I would appreciate it if this could be taken care of promptly. • Please feel free to call or email me if you need any further information. • If you need any help, contact me. (Less formal) • Let me know if you have any questions.

Complementary close

• Yours sincerely (UK), Sincerely (US)	(formal)
• Best Regards, Kind regards, Best wishes, Regards	(semi-formal and polite)
• Thank you, Best, Cheers, See you soon, All the best, Bye	(less formal but polite)

Signature

The closing is followed by your full name. It is beneficial to add your job position (if applicable), company name, and contact information. Use your email software to create a standard signature with complete contact information. Append it to every message. This looks professional and gives the recipient more options to contact you.	**Jessica Reed** *Sales Development Representative, Openplus* 669-221-6251 www.openplus.com Aaron Ross Finance Manager Envirotoner, Inc. 1550 Oceanview Avenue Tulsa, OK 74217 **Tel:** 918.555.6240 **Fax:** 918.555.6240 **Email:** aaronross@EnviroToner.net **Website:** wwww.EnbiroToner.net

Attachments

If you've attached a file to your email, make sure you mention it in the message (what it contains, and any actions needed).	*I've attached... / I'm attaching...* *Please find attached...*

Style and tone

A good professional email is brief, clear, professional, and polite. The tone of your email depends on your reader. The more distant the relationship is between you and your reader, the more formal the tone and expression must be.

Dos	Don'ts
Use short and clear sentences 　Keep your message brief and to the point. Use simple and straightforward sentences. **Use familiar and plain words** 　Simple and everyday words help our reader grasp your message. **Be conversational but professional** 　Keep your tone professional. When writing to someone you know well, write the way you are speak. **Be courteous and thoughtful** 　Make sure your tone is friendly, respectful and approachable.	• Use complex sentences and constructions. • Use overly formal words, trite expressions, clichés, and technical jargon. e.g. *as per your request, please be advised, acknowledge the receipt of.* • Use casual language, slang or abbreviations or business jargon that your recipients may not understand.　e.g."gotta" "*plz*"(please), "*LOL*" (laugh out loud) or "*BTW*" (by the way).

Layout

Dos	Don'ts
• Keep your email as concise as possible. • Use subheadings, numbers and bullets to streamline the information. • Leave spaces between paragraphs. • Use bold and italics to emphasize important points. • Keep your fonts classic.	• Use ALLCAPS as it is hard to read and considered shouting. • Use emoticons:-) (happy) or :-((sad). • Overuse exclamation points. • Don't use unusual font styles or colors until you are sure this is acceptable.

Business email etiquettes

- Consider your readers.
- Make your email easy to read and understand.
- Provide a clear, specific subject line.
- Use professional salutations.
- Include a signature block.
- Proofread every message before sending.
- Acknowledge receipt of messages promptly.
- Observe the common practices of your company.
- Don't use email to send confidential or sensitive information.
- Never send a rude or aggressive email.

Unit 6 Professional Emails

III E-mail Examples

There are certain phrases in email and letter writing that are particularly formal or particularly informal, and some are acceptable in both situations. Read the following email examples and look for words and phrases in the email that indicate the level of formality.

1. New employee welcome email.

This is an informal email welcoming the new employee and informing him what to expect on his first day. The tone is friendly and welcoming.

抄送	**To:** <HWOOD@widevalley.com> **From:** khanks@rainbow.com **Cc:**	E-mail address
主题	**Subject:** Welcome!	Subject
称呼	Dear Homer,	Salutation

正文	Welcome aboard! We are happy that you have finally decided to join Rainbow Corp. as a Production Planner. We are confident that your expertise and dedication can contribute significantly to the company.
	
	    You will have your employee orientation on Friday next week with our human resources personnel. She will discuss with you in detail our organizational chart, the products, and services of the company, employee benefits, and aspects of your job. She will also give you a tour around the office so you would get to know the other employees.
	
	    Once again, a warm welcome to you and we hope you have a good "stay".
		Message

祝语	Good luck! Kevin Hanks	Close
落款	———————————————	
电子邮件签名	Human Resources Specialist Rainbow Corp. 4300 Morales Highway San Padre, CA 95620-0326 http://rainbow.com	Signature block

2. Semi-formal email for notification of scheduled meeting.

This is the revised version of the email discussed in Case Study 1. The writer restructures the information and adjusts the style and tone so that the message is brief, clear, focused, natural, and easy to understand.

139

Dear all,

We will hold our monthly planning meeting at 4 p.m. on Thursday, March 12, in the small conference room. Each of us should be prepared to give an update on our current projects. We plan to discuss:

* work completed
* upcoming milestones
* project risks
* open issues

If you are unable to attend this meeting for any reason, please call Mary at extension 5555 by noon the day of the meeting.

Stephen King

3. Formal request email and its reply email.

This is a formal external email requesting a copy of invoice. Note how the writer uses indirect and polite expressions when making a request.

To: abc@wyz.com
CC: Accounts Payable
Subject: Request for copy of invoice
Dear ABC,

I'm LMN from the Accounts Payable department at GHI. Ltd. I understand that we have an invoice outstanding with your company since 07/01/2010. This email is to request you for a copy of the invoice, so that we can clear it for payment at the earliest.

First of all, apologies for the delay in payment. The accounts team has been reshuffled and this case came to my notice just an hour ago and I am writing to you immediately. The invoice in question is invoice number 246849, for Mr. JKI who stayed at your hotel for a period of 4 days. That is, from 06/28/2010 to 07/01/2010.

Please send it to the email address mentioned below so that I can issue the payment right away. Once again, sincere apologies for the delay.

Thank you,

LMN,
Senior Executive
Accounts Payable,

GHI. Ltd
accountspayable@ghi.com

Reply to request email

To: accountspayable@ghi.com
CC: Accounts Credit
Subject: FAO-LMN: Copy of invoice

Dear LMN,

This is in reference to the email that you sent me this morning. First off, I would like to thank you for taking the initiative of asking for the invoice copy.

As requested by you, I have attached a copy of the invoice 246849. I'm sure you have our bank details.

Thank you,
ABC,
Accounts Credit,
DYU Group of Hotels

4. Two request emails.

The following two emails are sent to people within an organization. The first one is written in a formal and respectful tone. The second one is less formal yet still polite and considerate.

Sick leave email (Formal)

Subject: Leave application
Dear Mr. Thompson,
I would like to bring to your kind attention that my doctor has advised me complete bed rest for 3 days due to high fever and chronic head ache. I am writing this application to serve as an official document supporting my leaves. I would be very grateful to you if you consider my application and grant me leave for 3 days starting from 20th August. I am attaching my medical reports for your reference.
I have explained everything to my team member regarding the current project and I am confident that he can handle the project well in my absence. I will be resuming my duties on 23rd August.

I appreciate your consideration and approval to my request. Thank you very much in advance

Best regards

Robert D Costa

Meeting request email (Informal)

Subject: Request to Meet on Saturday

Hello John,

I was wondering if we can meet at your earliest convenient time to discuss the dispute in my office. I apologize for the short notice but this is kind of an urgent matter.

Would Thursday, 15 June 3 p.m. suit you? If not, please let me know another time Thursday that could work.

Thank you very much for your time.

Best Regards

Pat Cashin

5. Two thank-you emails.

The first one is written for the professional purpose and thus it is formal and professional. The second one thanks a coworker, and the tone is informal and personal.

Thank-you email (More formal)

Dear Samantha,

On behalf of ABC Centre, I wish to express my gratitude towards you for the interesting and informative series of training workshops that you presented to our staff. Everyone found your sessions both useful and enjoyable.

We hope you will be able to provide workshops for our staff again next year.

Thank you again,

Sonia Rodriguez

Thank-you email (Less formal)

Hello Tom,

Just wanted you to know that I thought you did a terrific job updating the customer service database. Now that we have returning callers identified, we are building those necessary relationships with customers. It is far better than treating return customers as if we don't know who they are.

Again, bravo Tom, for a job well done. We really appreciate your efforts — as do the customers.

Thank you.
Tricia

6. Congratulation emails.

Congratulation email (Semi-formal)

Subject: Congratulations from ABC Company

Dear Ms. Mulai:

Please accept my congratulations on your promotion to Vice-President of ABC Ventures. I would like to wish you every success in your new position. I look forward to continued cooperation between our companies.

Sincerely yours,

Ryan Fisher
Managing Director
ABC Company

Congratulation email (Informal)

Subject: Congratulations from Margaret

Hi Johana,

Congratulations on your promotion! I'm very happy and sad at the same time, as we're no longer going to be working together. I'm sure you'll be a great success in your new job. Let's stay in touch.

Margaret

7. Complaint email (formal).

Subject: Complaint against your staff member "Henry Cooper"

Dear Mr. Moore,

I would like to lodge a complaint regarding the bad service received by one of your staff when I had visited your bank branch on 27th of March 2012. I am a saving account holder in your bank with my account number being 2390786.

I had visited the branch to deposit some money in my account. I was asked to wait by one of the customer service executives by the name Henry Cooper and above that I was not provided with a token. After waiting for fifteen minutes when I asked the customer service executive for help, he said that he was busy though he was not attending to any customer. I had to leave without being attended.

I would request you to take action against the staff or else I may have to close my account.

Regards,

Nathan Lee.

8. Apology email (formal)

Dear Mr. Lee,

I would like to apologize on behalf of my staff for the unsatisfactory service provided to you at our bank branch. This is in regards to your visit to our branch on 27th of March 2012.

I understand that Henry Copper was unhelpful in solving your issue that day when he was not otherwise occupied. I also understand your frustration at having not been properly treated after having waited for fifteen minutes.

At RNT, we strive to provide the best service to our customers. I know that on this occasion we have let you down, and for that we are very sorry. I would like to assure you that we are taking steps to prevent it from happening in the future. Thank you for bringing this issue to our attention.

We value our customers and ask you to please feel free to continue to provide feedback about our services. If you have any further questions or would like to discuss this matter further, please feel free to contact me at my personal number 555-123-5555. We look forward to continuing serving you as a valued customer.

Thank you for your valuable support.

Yours sincerely,

Jack Moore
Customer Service Manager

IV Writing skills

Writing catchy email subject lines

E-mail subject lines perform the same function as a headline by attracting attention and getting your email content a chance to be read. They should summarize the message instead of describing it. A good subject line should:

Be clear and specific about the topic of the email.

- Put the most important words at the beginning.
- Provide specific, useful information Include necessary details.
- Use key words from the message.
- Avoids one-word subject lines (e.g. Help, Lunch, or Urgent).

Be simple and concise.

- Keep it under 40 characters or about five to seven words.
- Skip articles, adjectives, and adverbs.
- Leave out unnecessary words.

How to write a subject line?

Ask yourself these questions before writing a subject line: *What's the core message or goal? What is the benefit to the reader? What words will convey this?* Then craft your subject line using this formula: [Topic] + [Essential details]. The topic can be a noun or gerund summarizing the message, followed by essential details related the topic.

e.g. **[Topic] + [Essential details]**

Collaboration in healthcare

Big news: New stores opening neat you

Inquiring about your design services

Follow the steps below:

(1) Write a complete sentence.

The company is going to collaborate with you on healthcare.

(2) Omit all the unnecessary words.

The company is going to collaborate with you on healthcare.

(3) Rearrange the word order (if necessary).

healthcare collaborate

(4) Change the part of speech (if necessary).

Healthcare collaboration / Collaboration in healthcare

Compare the following subjects

Bad Subject Lines	Good Subject lines
Meeting (vague and general)	Meeting Oct. 11 (specific and concise)
Meeting for March 12, Schedule, Guest List, Lunch and requests (too long, multiple topics)	Meeting about social media strategy - 10 a.m. March 12 (informative and focused)
IMPORTANT!!! (impolite, all caps and exclamation points)	Important – Meeting date changed (clear)
[blank subject line] (inconsiderate and unprofessional)	Employee evaluation. Reply by Friday (direct and clear)
Re: Re: Re: Employee Evaluation (repeated use of the same subject)	Final version of employee evaluation (clear and specific)

Task 4. Work in groups and discuss how to compose the subject lines based on the excerpts of email messages.

(1) Subject: _____

It is to inform you that we are continuously receiving late supplies from your end. Due to this delay we have bare huge loses last month.

We are continuously in contact with Mr. Usman but because of his false commitments, we are not receiving orders on time. From now on in-case of any delay your order will be cancelled and returned.

(2) Subject: _____

Thank you for taking the time to interview me today about the Marketing Coordinator role. It was great to meet with you and learn more about the position. I truly believe my skills and insights could add a lot to your team and together we could help the company surpass its goals.

(3) Subject: _____

We at San Joaquin are excited to be hosting this year's educational meeting, and I am excited to be able to formally invite you to the meeting we've termed "Dream Big 2014" at the Morales Gymnasium, San Joaquin High School on June 5, 2014, 2p.m..

(4) Subject: _____

I'm writing this mail on behalf of my team who were ought to submit you the assigned project by the specified deadline. Please accept my sincere apologies for all the inconveniences caused to you due to the late submission of the allotted work.

(5) Subject: _____

This is to inform you that our company is planning a get together on 11th April, Saturday, at 1 100 hours at Golden Beach Resorts. You may bring your spouses and children.

Making the email message easy to read

A good email should be easy to read and understand. Given that most people merely scan email messages instead of reading them word for word, you should try to present your email message for easy scanning. Keep it simple and sweet **(KISS)**.

Professional emails are not formal letters and should not be excessively long. Neither are they text messages, so they should not be meatless. Use the following methods to keep your message concise the scannable:

• **Keep the content clear and focused.** Put the most important information up top and make sure the message is focused on one goal.

• **Use short paragraphs.** Your reader may not get your point if your important details are buried in the middle of a long, thick paragraph. Break large blocks of text down into short paragraphs, each containing two or three sentences.

• **Use short sentences and understandable expressions.**

• **Use bulleted lists or numbered lists where necessary.** Lists make it easy for readers to skip large blocks of text and still get the key information quickly. Note that all the items on the list should be parallel in form.

• **Use white space.** Use a blank line between two paragraphs to make information easy to grasp.

• **Use headings.** Headings summarize the content and grab readers' attention.

• **Use boldface, underscoring and icons** where appropriate.

e.g.

From	Mary Samuels <mary.samuels@xya-inc.com>
To	Joan Smith <joan.smith@xyz-inc.com>
Subject	Tomorrow's meeting

Joan,
Before the meeting tomorrow, could you please do the following:
• Run through my PowerPoint slides one last time to check for typos.
• Speak to Matt to see whether he will be able to arrange a podium. If he can't get one, perhaps you could talk to Facilities and see whether they have one there.
• Get a remote clicker from Janet or Joe.
Thank you,
Mary

Bullet points also make it easier for you to reply to the bulleted items. You can just insert your responses under the bulleted items, utilizing a different font and color.

e.g.

> ...
> • Increase bid price by 20%
> *How about we do 10% instead for the first round?*
> • Improve final output by 100 units
> *Agree! We can do that!*
> • Reduce time to market by 3 months
> *Too tight - but think we can reduce to 2 months if supplier approves. Can you verify?*
> ...

Task 5. Read the email message below and rewrite it to make it easy to scan and understand. Try the following ways: ① Divide it into 2~4 shorter paragraphs; ② Use lists, white space, and a heading to organize information; ③ Improve the subject line.

(Original message)

To: juanlopez@example.com, robertconwey@example.com, sallywang@example.com
Subject: Project
Dear XYZ Project Team Member, Welcome to XYZ Project. I look forward to working with each of you. The XYZ Project will be starting soon. I will be heading up this project. I need to set some ground rules for project meetings. First of all, you must be on time for team meetings and full attendance of all team meetings is required unless a case of emergency. Moreover, all team members send the team leader their issues before the meeting and the agenda will be distributed before the meeting. Finally, you should inform the team leader if you're unable to complete work on time. Once again, welcome to XYZ Project. Let me know if you have any questions. Sincerely, Laura XYZ Project Team Lead

(Revised message)

To: juanlopez@example.com, robertconwey@example.com , sallywang@example.com
Subject:
Dear XYZ Project Team Member,   Sincerely, Laura XYZ Project Team Lead

Using the right style and tone

1. Think about how formal you should to be.

An email at work is a business document, thus you should keep your writing professional. However, depending on the recipient, the style of your email may vary. The more distant the relationship is between you and your recipient, the more formal the tone and expression must be. Here are the general rules about when to use a formal style or less formal email style:

Use a formal email style:

• if you do not know the recipients well

• if you send an email to someone who is above you in authority such as your boss or a teacher

• if you write to a company you're doing business with

• if it is required in your organization

Use a less formal email style:

• if you write to a business colleague who is well-known to you and / or on friendly terms

• if it is encouraged in your organization (your boss and others use an informal style)

• if you write a personal email that contains both business and non-business topics

More Formal (for business letters or formal emails)	Less Formal (for informal emails)
Dear Mr. Smith, I am writing to thank you for all your help. Unfortunately, I will not be able to attend the meeting. I look forward to seeing you next week. Sincerely, Tim Jackson	Hi John, Many thanks for your help. Sorry, I can't make it. See you next week. Cheers, Tim

Many workplaces are moving towards a more informal communication style. People prefer semi-formal or informal business emails. You can just write the way you speak. However, you should refrain from getting too informal before you get to know the recipient better. If you're not sure whether you should use a formal email or an informal email, it's often safer to use a more formal style.

However, it is important to note that people in different countries have different perceptions about the level of formality in email writing. For example, in USA, Spain or Greece, emails are usually short, informal, direct and to the point. They see this as being efficient and productive. Yet the same type of emails will be perceived as rude and thoughtless in countries like France and Germany, where email correspondence is expected to be highly formal, much like a written business letter.

2. Think about how direct or polite you want to be.

Make sure your tone is friendly and polite. Depending on the recipient, consider how direct or polite you want the message to be. Consider these techniques for being indirect and tentative:

(1) **Modal verbs:** *might, can, could, would*

(2) **Questions:** *Would you mind...? Is it possible...? Could you please...?*

(3) **Distancing phrases** (not using the present tense): *I was hoping..., I was wondering..., I wanted to...*

(4) **Tentative language:** *Maybe..., Perhaps..., I'm not sure if..., I don't know if..., I'm afraid..., I regret that..., I'm sorry that...*

(5) **Introductory phrases:** *It looks like..., It seems like..., Actually...,To be honest...Well..., I see what you're saying (but...)*

(6) **Positive language** (avoiding negative expressions like "bad" "won't work" "ineffective" etc.): *It might not be the best approach.*

Direct / Straightforward	Indirect / Polite
I want to be excused from Monday's tutorial.	Would it be possible to be excused from Monday's tutorial?
I need this in half an hour.	I was hoping that I could have this in half an hour.
There will be a delay.	I'm afraid there may be a slight delay.
It's a bad idea	To be honest, I'm not sure if that would be a good idea.
Please clarify if this price includes delivery.	Could you possibly clarify for example if this price includes delivery?
We delay 24 hours because of the storm.	I'm very sorry, but we have a delay of 24 hours because of the storm.
This is terrible work.	This could be improved.
I disagree.	I'm of a different opinion. / I see it differently.
I don't like it.	I'd prefer... / It's not my cup of tea.
I can't find your application.	I've looked on your website, but I can't seem to find the application for...

Task 6. Make the following expressions more formal or less informal.

Make the following expressions more formal.

(1) What do you need? _____

(2) I'm sorry to tell you that ... _____

(3) Don't forget that ... _____

(4) I promise ... _____

(5) Could you ...? _____

(6) I need to ... _____

Make the following expressions less formal.

(7) Thank you for your email dated... _____

(8) I will take the necessary action to solve this issue. _____

(9) Please accept my apologies for …
(10) As per your request, attached please find…
(11) Do not hesitate to contact me if you have any further questions or concerns.

Task 7. Look at the following situations. Decide how formal and direct the email should be and write the sentences for making requests or suggestions accordingly.

(1) You ask your subordinate to send you the sales figures of the second quarter before Friday afternoon.

(2) You want to meet with your manager for 20 minutes to talk about your suggestions about how to increase sales.

(3) You have some personal issues you need to take care of on Monday morning. You write to your supervisor to take Monday morning off and make up the time later in the week.

(4) You have got a job offer, but you write to the employer that you want to turn down the job offer due to some personal reasons.

(5) You write to remind a young colleague that she has make some mistakes on the invoice.

Task 8. Rewrite the following formal business letter as a less formal email to someone you know well. Use these phrases in your email: *I just have a few questions about, can you, also, asked for, haven't, get back to me with the information as soon as possible.*

Dear Mr Mitchell,

I am writing in reference to the current situation with the Skipton Airport Project. We have a number of questions which we hope you could answer.

First of all, could you please provide us with an update on where you are on the Skipton Airport Project. We would also appreciate it if you could clarify what the current issues with the delivery system are, and confirm when you expect them to be resolved.

In addition, at the end of our last meeting we requested a copy of the latest project update report. Unfortunately, we have still not received it. We would appreciate it if you could forward this to us.

I would really appreciate it if you could deal with these matters urgently.

I look forward to hearing from you.

Yours sincerely,

Ian McAdam
Development Manager

Task 9. Rewrite the following informal email by replacing the underlined informal phrases with more formal ones.

Hi Joe,

<u>Thanks</u> for your email received last night.

<u>Just a quick note</u> to confirm our appointment on March 11. My flight gets in about 8 p.m.. <u>Any chance</u> somebody could pick me up at the airport?

<u>Don't forget to</u> attach the brochure of your new research center. I'll visit it on March 11.

<u>See you</u> next week.

Simon Jones

V Exercises and Practice

Task 10. The following are some abbreviations, acronyms and initialisms in business writing. Write their meanings and decide whether they are appropriate in the body of a business letter or email. Use a "Y" for appropriate and "N" for inappropriate.

asap _____	Encl. _____	Att. _____	FYI _____
BTW _____	tks _____	FAQs _____	Bcc _____
c/o _____	n/a _____	PS _____	LOL _____
TTYL _____	G2G _____	CU _____	L8R _____

Writing the email header and subject line

Task 11. Complete the email headers below according to the situations.

(1) You need to email Jeff Green, the Personnel Manger, about banning smoking in the company. Jeff's email address is J. Green@personnel.CivilandCivic.com. The message needs to be copied to the Office Manager, Susan Clark. Her address is S_Clark@admin.CivilandCivic.com.

(2) You need to send last year's sales figures to John Doe, the Sales Manager. The message is also sent to Mary Smith and Sam Jones for information purposes only. But you do not want to make their addresses visible to John Doe. Their addresses are: john_doe@jones.com, mary_smith@jones.com, and sam_jones@jones.com.

Message 1

Send	Save As Draft	Cancel
To:		
Cc:		
Bcc:		
Subject:		

Message 2

Send	Save As Draft	Cancel
To:		
Cc:		
Bcc:		
Subject:		

Writing the opening and closing paragraphs

Task 12. Sarah has written four emails. Match each opening line of the email in the left column to the corresponding situation in the right column. Consider how the purpose and audience determine the style of language.

(1) Dear Mr. Smith,
This is to confirm I have received your email.

(2) Dear Sir or Madam:
Could you please send me…?

(3) Hi there Sue.
Hope you're well. Might be a bit late on Saturday…

(4) Dear Mr. Morgan,
I am writing to you because I am worried that…

(5) Dear staff members,
Greetings! This is to inform you that our company is planning…

A. Sarah emails all the staff in her company to invite them to the company's annual picnic.

B. Sarah writes to her friend about their plans to shop at the weekend.

C. Sarah emails someone she doesn't know asking for more information about the product.

D. Sarah emails the husband of a colleague at the department. She wants to know why his wife was absent and out of contact.

E. Sarah replies an email form ABC Company to notify them that you have seen their email.

Task 13. Imagine you are Sarah Jones. Write a closing paragraph for each email in the above exercise.

(1) _____
(2) _____
(3) _____
(4) _____
(5) _____

Unit 6 Professional Emails

Putting it together

Task 14. Choose the correct words and phrases to complete the following emails.

A) I am writing about	B) We would like to announce	C) I would like to confirm
D) Thank you for	E) Further to your last email	F) This email is regarding
G) I was pleased	H) I am sorry to inform you	I) For more for formation
J) don't hesitate to contact me	K) Thank you once again for	L) I wish
M) I would like to take this opportunity		N) I / We look forward to seeing you.
O) express my deepest appreciation for		

---

1. Announcement email

From: Michael Manning [M-Manning@AWC.com]
To: AWC Mailing list
Subject: Annual Asia Women's Conference

_____ (1) the annual Asia Women's Conference will be held from June 15 – 17 at the Garden Hotel, located in 118 Gloucester Rd, Wan Chai, Hong Kong. _____ (2) about the conference, including our sponsoring hotel information, seminar descriptions, and relevant maps, please visit <u>www.asi.com/conference/hongkong</u>.

Please send a confirmation of your attendance by April 10 with the subject title "AWC Confirmation". Please include your name and number of guests for hotel rooms. _____(3).
Sincerely

Michael Manning
Conference Director

---

2. Confirmation email

From: Susan Ashworth [susan-ashworth@gmail.com]
To: Michael Manning [M-Manning@AWC.com
Subject: AWC Confirmation

Dear Mr. Manning,

_____ (4) the information about the conference. I am really looking forward to the great seminar and learning more about Hong Kong.

_____ (5) three people will be attending this year's conference:
Susan Ashworth
Mary Sinati
Boris Peter

I would like to reserve two double rooms. Please send me all the relevant registration materials as soon as possible.

_____ (6) inviting me. I look forward to hearing from you.

Best regards,

Susan Ashworth

153

(Continued)

3. Thank you email / Good news email	4. Refusal email / Bad news email
Dear Mr. Bale: _____ (7) to thank you and other employees of United Way for the exceptional effort that you have put into taking this company to the heights that it is at right now. With Labor Day just a few days away, I feel that it is the perfect occasion to _____ (8) all that you have done for your department, and the company. Since Labor Day this year is on a Friday, _____ (9) all of you a happy long weekend as well, and hope that you will have a wonderful time with your family and friends. To make this deal sweeter, I will be announcing a bonus for each employee on our first working day after the weekend. Have a wonderful Labor Day and a rocking weekend. Thank you very much. Evan Robertson CEO United Way	Good Afternoon Peter, _____ (10) to receive your proposal for the design of the company's website. Your proposal was very professional and well-thought out. After careful consideration, _____ (11) that we decided to accept the proposal of another employee with lower estimated costs. I do personally like your proposal and we will be more than happy to consider you for any web development or redesign projects we have in the future. If you want to discuss this matter further, _____ _____ (12) on my mobile, 676 005 451. Take care, David Mitchell Project Manager

Task 15. Complete the following emails by translating the expressions in the brackets into English.

(1) **E-mail announcing a meeting — Neutral** (This email also asks the recipients to reply whether they can attend).

Subject: July research meeting

Dear all,

_____ (通知各位参加) our monthly research meeting in the conference room at 10 a.m. on Friday, July 16.

John and Jane will report on the meeting with their French counterparts. _____ _____ (每人需准备汇报项目的最新进展).

If there's anything you would like to discuss in the meeting, _____ (请给我发

邮件) and I'll include it in the meeting's agenda.

_____ (请尽快回复能否参加会议).

　　Regards,

　　David Mitchell

　　IT Project Manager

(2) **E-mail confirming attendance at the meeting — Informal** (A suggestion is offered in this email reply to the meeting invitation).

　　Hi David,

　　Thanks for your email. _____(我确定能够参加) the July 16 meeting. I've phoned all team members to get their input and will be prepared to summarize their comments to the group.

_____(我想建议另外两个会议的议题):

　　① Hiring and training new research analysts

　　② Vote on budgeting priorities.

　　Kind regards

　　Francis

(3) **E-mail confirming attendance at the meeting — Neutral** (The invited guest responses to the meeting invitation).

Dear Mr Mitchell.

_____(感谢你们的邀请). I would like to confirm my attendance at the meeting _____ (定于) for this Friday, at 10 a.m. on the 16th of July.

_____
_____(我一定按您要求做好报告，在会上发言). I will make sure to furnish you a copy a few days before we meet to give you some time to review the contents and alert me to any changes that have to be done if needed.

_____(期待与您相见) on 16 July.

　　Sincerely

　　John Doe

(4) **E-mail declining an invitation to the meeting apologizing for absence from the meeting — Formal** (The invited guest responds to the invitation).

Dear Mr Mitchell,

_____(很高兴收到您的邀请) to the meeting on July 16. I am truly honored. _____, _____ (遗憾的是，由于) a prior commitment on the same day, _____(我无法参加会议).

_____(我为由

155

此带来的不便表示道歉).

_____ (如果您需要了解更多信息，尽管与我联系).

　　Yours sincerely,
　　Adélard Matombe

(5) E-mail replying the above email — Neutral (This email is to persuade the recipient to attend the meeting).
Dear Mr. Matombe,

_____ (感谢您的回复).

_____ (我理解) you're very busy at the moment. As I said in the invitation I sent you, in the meeting we're going to be looking at the problems we've had with the current projects. To be honest, we still don't know the full extent. That's the reason why we felt that your attendance was necessary.

_____ (如果您能重新考虑参加这个会议，我们将不胜感激).

　　Regards,
　　David Mitchell
　　IT Project Manager

(6) E-mail apologizing for not attending the meeting — Informal.
Hi David,

_____ (我恐怕不能参加这周五的会了).omething very important _____ (刚刚发生) and I'm going to be very busy this week.

_____ (抱歉通知得很仓促). but I just found out this morning.

_____ (能不能把会议挪到下周召开呢？) ?

_____ (如果可以的话请告诉我).

　　Regards
　　Jane

(7) E-mail responding to the request.
Hi Jane,

_____ (谢谢你告诉我) that you can't attend the meeting on July 16.

I've spoken to the other attendees (John Doe, Daniels, David Mitchell, etc.) and _____ _____ _____ (我们一致同意把会议调到更适合你的一个日期和时间).

Please advise me of a time and a date which is more suitable for your schedule.

Regards,

David

(8) E-mail for Sending Minutes of Meeting — Formal.

Subject: Minutes of the Meeting dated July 16, 2017

Greetings!

This email is _____ (关于) the research meeting that took place in the conference room at 10 a.m. on July 16. _____ (请查看附件中的会议记录，回顾本次会议).

If there are any questions or concerns _____ (关于文件内容), please feel free to contact me.

Sincerely

Renee Portman

Executive Secretary

Formality of language

Task 16. Formal emails use different phrases and expressions from informal emails. Decide whether the following expressions are more formal or less informal and put them into the right box.

	Formal	Informal
Reasons for writing	I am emailing you regarding / with regard to the …	This is to confirm / reserve / invite…
Making requests		
Apologizing		
Making complaints		
Making arrangements		
Offering help		

(1) Drop me a line if you need more info. / Let me know if you want me to lend you a hand (with…) / Give me a call if you want any help (with…). / If you've got any questions, feel free to ask.

(2) Sorry for causing these problems / We want to say sorry / Sorry about…

(3) I regret to say that I was not completely satisfied with… / I am writing to express my dissatisfaction with… / Unfortunately, … did not meet the high standards that I expected. / I trust

this matter can be resolved very quickly.

(4) I am writing to inform / confirm / reserve / enquire / invite… / With reference to our telephone conversation on Friday, I would like to… / Thank you for your email of …concerning the…

(5) I'd like to ask you… / Would you…? / I need… / I want you to… / Is it alright (for me) to…? / Can I…? / Make sure… / Don't forget to…

(6) Do you mind if I…? / Is it possible for … to…? / Would it be acceptable for me to…? / Do I have your permission to…?

I was wondering if … / Could you possibly…? / I'd greatly appreciate it if… / I would be grateful if… / I would like to request…

(7) I'm writing to tell you about… / Just a quick note to tell you that… / I'd like to ask… / Just checking in to make sure that…

(8) Would you be available…? / … if that is convenient with you. / Would it be possible for you to meet this afternoon? / You can suggest a time of your convenience for…

(9) …wasn't good enough. / … was terrible. / I want to complain about… / I am very angry about…

(10) I am writing to apologize for… / Please accept my apologies for… / I apologize for the delay in replying to your email.

(11) Are you free…? / … is best for me. / Sorry, I can't make it. / Do you have time to meet this afternoon?

(12) I am willing to… / Please contact me if I can be of any assistance. / It is our great pleasure to offer you. / Please do not hesitate to contact me should you require any further assistance / information.

Write concisely

Task 17. Good business writing is concise, direct, and unambiguous.

Make the sentences more concise by eliminating wordiness or using shorter sentences.

(1) The motivation of staff has been ensured by introducing lunch talks.

(2) The chairman came to a conclusion that we need to make an improvement over the system.

(3) We currently have several available job openings for a variety of positions in our R&D department.

(4) We are now in the process of evaluating how to address the issue that exists regarding the performance of our team members.

Concise writing

1. Eliminate wordy, redundant or superfluous expressions (e.g. "at this point in time" "personal opinion").
2. Eliminate clichés (e.g. put it in a nutshell; better late than never).
3. Reduce nominalizations. Convert the noun into a verb (e.g. give an analysis — analyze).
4. Avoid passive voice.
5. Avoid expletives (e.g. "there is" "there are").
6. Break long sentences into shorter sentences.

(5) In spite of the fact that our budget for advertising is now higher, our sales figures have not gotten any better.

(6) In recognition of the necessity of better staff training, the company made a decision on the recruitment of a Training Director.

(7) The reason why we failed to reply is that we were not apprised of the fact until yesterday that somehow the report had been unavoidably delayed.

Assignments

1. Write professional emails.

Work in pairs. Choose Task A or Task B for the following situations. Write an email to the person concerned, following the guidelines for writing professional email discussed in this unit. Your email should contain all the elements of an email message. Exchange your email with your partner for feedback. Revise the document and send the final, revised document to the teacher.

Situation 1: A — Write a request email to your colleague.

You are the project leader of Project Omega at a paper products company. You have come across some roadblocks, so you want to hold a project status meeting to discuss the work on August 13 at 10 a.m. in the Harpers Conference Room. Because you need the suggestions and feedback from a marketing point of view, you want to invite Ms. Cortez, the marketing manager, to attend the meeting. Write an email to her asking her if the date and time work for her. The outline of the project plan will be attached with this email.

Situation 1: B — Respond to your partner's email.

You are Ms. Cortez, the marketing manager. You have just received an email message requesting a meeting. You are busy on the suggested day. Reply the email, agree to meet, but suggest another time. Give a reason why you are not available then.

Situation 2: A — Write a goodwill email to all employees.

You are Bob Shaffer, the General Manager of Evertech Corporation Limited. With the New Year just a few days away, you email all the employees to thank them for their great work and wish them a happy holiday. You also announce a holiday bonus for each employee will be included in their paychecks this month.

Situation 2: B — Write a goodwill email to your boss.

You are James Gordon, the Marketing Manager of Evertech Corporation Limited. Before the beginning of a new year, you write a Happy New Year email to your boss, Bob Shaffer, to express your greetings and gratitude on behalf of the team. Since your team will gather for coffee Starbucks at on the last working day, you also invite your boss to join to celebrate the new year.

Situation 3: A — Write an inquiry email.

You are Frank Rosling working at Berlin Energies. You saw a conference poster on 2018 Even Information Website. Your company needs to book a stand in the conference exhibition center. Write an inquiry email to ask for more information about the conference and exhibitors.

> **Global Electricity Conference**
> The largest meeting place for energy industry professionals from over 100 countries worldwide.
>
> > San Paolo International Conference
> > and Exhibition Centre
> > 17-19 February

Situation 3: B — Respond to the inquiry email.

You are Amy Natera, the Conference Programme Manager. Respond to the inquiry email from Berlin Energies. Explain to Frank Rosling that while all the stands for the exhibition have been booked. Ask him to fill in the attached form with the company details if he agrees to put the company on a waiting list in case space becomes available at the last minute.

2. Check and evaluate emails.

Us the following checklist to revise and polish the emails you write. Exchange your email with your partner. Evaluate your partner's email, pointing out its strengths and weaknesses.

E-mail writing checklist

• **Subject line:** Provide a clear, specific subject line.
• **Salutation:** Use professional salutations.
• **Body:** Properly starting an email (Direct vs. Indirect approach).
A body that is clear, direct, and to the point (avoid any sort of ambiguity).
A body that, if written as a reply, addresses all items brought up by the email that you are responding to.
• **Sign-off:** Sign off politely and appropriately.
Include a signature block with your name and position at the bottom.
• **Layout:** Use white space, bullet lists and short paragraphs to make your email easy to read and understand.
• **Style and tone:** An overall professional and conversation style; not too informal nor too overly formal.
Polite, friendly, and positive tone.
• **Proofread:** Check spelling and grammar.
Comments   Anything that could be improved?   Anything that you particularly like?

Unit 7 Professional Memos

> Hardcopy memos and e-memos are commonplace written documents in the workplace. Memos are typically used for communicating inside an organization. They are important for communicating policies, changes of policy, confirmation and acknowledgments, and notices of events or urgent company news. This unit introduces different types of memos, the main components of a memo, and the memo writing guidelines.

Objectives

After completing this unit, you will be able to

◆ Identify the parts of business memos;
◆ Identify different types of business memos;
◆ Understand the basic qualities that contribute to a good memo;
◆ Compose professional quality memos.

 I Pre-class activities

Research and Explore

Task 1. Memo is used for different purposes as a quick form of internal communication of an organization. Search the internet for examples of workplace memos. Summarize the functions or purposes of memos in the workplace and describe how these purposes affect the organization of the memo message.

_____
_____
_____
_____

📣 Case study

Task 2. Sarah Jones has received a memo from the General Manager asking for cost saving ideas for the company. Sarah is going to respond to the memo below with a cost-saving proposal, i.e. a duplex printing policy. She believes this policy would allow the company to save money by asking all staff to print on both sides of paper where possible.

> FROM: Daniel Smith, General Manager
> TO: All Department Heads
> DATE: August 16, 2017
> Subject: Cost Saving Ideas
>
> In preparation for the managers' meeting, I want to know your opinions about how to reduce costs for our company.
>
> Please respond this week. I need a short proposal.

What factors would she consider when composing the memo so that the general manager will understand and accept her proposal more easily? Use the following questions to help her plan the memo.

Purpose: Why is she writing the memo? What is the problem she will address?

Audience: Who is the audience of the memo? What kind of information does the audience need? What are the questions / concerns the audience may have?

Organization: How should the information organized? (Opening, middle, closing paragraphs)

Style and Tone: What kind of style and tone should she use?

☞ See "Introduction" and "Writing skills" in Section Ⅱ and Section Ⅳ for help.

Ⅱ Introduction

A memo is a business document that is used to correspond internally within an organization. The term memo is short for memorandum. The plurals are memoranda and memos. Memos are written to get someone to do something or inform them about important information. They are often sent as attachments to emails or are posted on the bulletin board or company intranets for all employees to see. Electronic memos are most commonly referred to as e-memos. Memos tend to be less formal than letters and may be written in a more conversational tone.

Memos are written for a wide variety of internal purposes — for example, to make announcements, outline policies, discuss procedures, report on company activities, update work on a project, transmit meeting minutes, request information, and encourage employees to take the action. From brief research reports and progress reports to trip reports and thumb nail proposals, the memo form is widely used to communicate technical and administrative information. Memos frequently address a small or large group of people, but some of the memos you write may be intended for one person.

Parts of a Memo

Memos are generally divided into two parts: the heading and the body. Memos do not include a formal salutation or complimentary closing; instead, they use "To" "From" "Date" and "Subject" headings. Note: The "To" line eliminates the need for a salutation like 'Dear Mr. David' in the message. Most organizations have a memo template or standard format that employees can use.

Part		Writing tips	Example
Heading	Title 标题 Company logo (optional)	The word "**Memo**" or "**Memorandum**" is centered at the top of the page. A preprinted company name and logo may appear above the word "Memo". Often a company uses a preprinted memo sheet.	**Valley Transportation Authority** MEMORANDUM
	To 收件人	The names of everyone who will receive the memo. For **informal memos**, use the receiver's given name or use the first initial and last name of each recipient if all recipients know each other's names and positions.	*To: Raymond* *To: R Hunt*
		For **formal memos**, memos to superiors, or if everyone on the list does not know each other, include the first and last name and title or department of the recipient.	*To: Raymond Hunt, Marketing Executive* *To: Dr. Steve Kent, Ext. 157* *To: All Customer Service Personnel*

		When sending a memo to more than one person, either separate them by commas or list them.	*To: Bill White, John Smith, Susan Taylor*
			To: Bill White
			    John Smith
			    Susan Taylor

		If the receiver's list is too long to fit in the "To" line, use the phrase "See distribution list" and place the names at the end of the memo.	*To: Distribution list* *To: See the distribution list on page 2*
	From 发件人	The name of the writer. There is no complimentary close or signature line, but you may initial your name here.	*From: B. White* *B.W.*
		For informal memos, use the sender's first name.	*From: Bill*
		For more formal memos, use the sender's full name and professional title.	*From: Bill White, Coordinator* *From: Bill White, Ext. 690*

(Continued)

Heading	**Date** 日期	Complete and current date • Avoid using numbers for months and days. Write the month as a word or an abbreviation. • To avoid confusion between the British and American date systems.	*Date: January 7, 2013* *Date: 5 April 2018*
	Subject / Re 主题／事由	Summary of what the memo is about. Should be clear, concise and to the point. Should be restricted to one topic or idea.	*Subject: Thanksgiving weekend schedule* *Re: Tobacco Use Policy*
	CC 抄送	This is for others you might want to read the memo.	*CC: Jim Bobby*
	Second-page (optional) 第二页标题	When the memo exceeds one page, begin the second and subsequent pages with the page number, recipient's name, and date.	*Page 2* *Raymond Hunt* *January 7, 201*

Body	**Message** 正文	**Short memos:**
		  Introduction – States the purpose of the memo / summarize the topic / Gives the background information
		  Body – Provides details relevant to the purpose
		  Close / Conclusion – Briefly states the conclusion or expected action. Or ends the memo on a positive note.
			I am sending this memo in response to…
			
			As you are all aware, …
			Let me know if you have any questions or concerns.

		Long memos:
		  Memos longer than two pages generally have a more formal structure than shorter ones. A long memo should have the following sections:
			Situation *Introduction*
			Problem *Background*
			Solution *Discussion*
			Actions *Conclusion*
			           Recommendation

	Signature (optional) 签名	Place this information three lines from the page top and begin your text three lines below.	*page 2. Allen Raines* *20 January 2000*
		Does not need to be signed. A writer may sign in one of the following ways. ① Sign or initial your name at the bottom of the memo the sender's full name _____ more formal. the sender's handwritten name _____ more friendly ② Sign your initials by the typed name in the "From" line. ③ Sign in a line provided under typed the name in the heading to show that you approve the contents of the memo or to authenticate the letter. Note: MLT and rjm are initials. The signature means MLT dictated a memo that rjm typed.	*Karen Mills* *MLT: rjm* *cc: D Jones* *To: Terry Collin* *From: Bill Williams* *B. W.* *Date: October 25, 2010* *Subject: July Trade Fair*

(Continued)

Body	Reference Initials (optional) 打字员姓名缩写	The initials of the typist. Uses lower case and appears below the last paragraph. You should not include reference initials if you key the memo yourself.	*km*
	Attachment / Enclosure (optional) 附件	Tells the recipient that a document is included with the memo.	*Enclosure: Travel cheque* *Attachments: Contract*

Style and tone

Memos are characterized by being brief, direct, and easy to navigate. A good memo should be:

• **Short and concise**

Conciseness is desired in memos more than in letters. Make your sentences, paragraphs, and overall memo as brief and as focused as possible. While memo length is determined by purpose and audience, typically a business memo is no longer than one page. Wordy expressions and sentences should be avoided.

• **Professional and easy to read**

Memos are usually less formal than letters but should maintain a professional, succinct style. You should choose familiar and conversational words, especially when you write e-memos. Abbreviations and acronyms are used sometimes.

However, memos that convey "official" information such as announcements, policies or procedures are more formal in tone. So are the memos addressed to people above the writer's rank.

• **Direct**

Memos are always direct, and the purpose is clearly announced in the subject line and the first paragraph.

• **Courteous**

Polite language is used no matter what the receiver's level in the organization. Develop the "you attitude".

• **Objective**

Memos are a place for just the facts, and should have an objective tone without personal bias, preference, or interest on display. Avoid subjectivity.

Types of memos

There are different types of memos you might have to write, each with its own organizational format.

In terms of the function, memos may be:

Informational memos, also known as informative memos, which provide or convey information such as company announcements, policy changes, promotions, personnel changes, or a project status update.

Instructional memos, or request memos, which call for and expect an action to be taken. For instance, they are used to request employees to attend a meeting, to make changes to work procedures or practices, or to address a problem, such as employee tardiness or absence.

Memo reports, or internal short reports, which are written on memo paper and follow the memo format. They are longer than the conventional memo (two pages or more) and are therefore divided into separate, labelled sections.

In terms of the directions of communication, memos can be categorized into:

• **Downward flow of memos** (from superiors to subordinates) Announcements, policy, requests, procedures, etc..

• **Upward flow of memos** (from subordinates to superiors) Requests, responses, reports, etc..

• **Horizontal flow of memos** (between employees or colleagues) Requests, responses, reports, etc..

III Resume examples

1. An informational memo (downward) addressed to all staff announcing a decision.

MEMORANDUM		Heading
TO: All Staff		
FROM: Ray Courson RC		
DATE: November 9th, 2015		Body
SUBJECT: STAFF CHRISTMAS PARTY		

It's that time of year again. As you all know, Christmas is our busiest season of the year. Every year it is a struggle for management and supervisors to find the time and energy to organize a staff Christmas party. This year, we have decided to postpone the Christmas party until after our busy season.	Purpose: Uses the indirect approach to put the bad news in the end of paragraph 1
Party Details • Date: Second or third Saturday in January (T.B.A) • Theme: Beach • Food: Caribbean • Special events: Karaoke and belly dancing	Message: Important details are put in a separate paragraph with bullet lists
We apologize that the celebration will have to wait until the new year, but we guarantee that it will be worth the wait. Anyone interested in volunteering to help out with the event is encouraged to call Lucy, our events coordinator. Lucy's cell phone number is 222-3098. Please contact Lucy outside of business hours regarding this matter. Thank you.	Conclusion: Calls to action
Enclosure	Enclosure notation

2. An instructional memo (downward) addressed to multiple people calling for an action to take.

GREENHUT CONSTRUCTION COMPANY, INC. ESTABLISHED 1946 **MEMO** **TO:** Distribution List Below **FROM:** Larry Northup, Executive Vice President **RE:** Subcontractor Employee Leasing **DATE:** December 10th, 2013 Effective today, we will require you to report any contract labor sources (employee leasing) to be used on each Greenhut project. At the beginning of each project we will ask you to provide written notice of labor sources you plan to use. For projects started before today's date, we ask you to provide written notice of any labor sources you are using or plan to use. You will need to begin providing lien waivers for these labor sources with your next pay application. If you have any questions or concerns, please feel free to contact me at our office (850)433-5421. LN/mt cc: All Subcontractors Greenhut Project Managers Greenhut Superintendents	**Heading** Distribution list is used when the memo is sent to a group pf people **Body** Introduction: Introduces the main point Discussion: Presents the secondary information Conclusion: Requests actions Reference initials Distribution list is put here showing all the intended recipients.

3. An informational memo (upward) delivering bad news in formal and polite tone.

MEMO **To:** Katherine Chu, Regional Manager **From:** Stephen Yu, Sales *SY* **Date :** 5 April 2018 **Subject:** My resignation I am writing to inform you of my intention to resign from G & S Holdings. I have appreciated very much my four years working for the company. The training has been excellent and I have gained valuable experience working within an efficient and professional team environment. In particular, I have appreciated your personal guidance during these first years of my career. I feel now that it is time to further develop my knowledge and skills base in a different environment. I would like to leave, if possible, in a month's time on Saturday, 5 May. This will allow me to complete my current workload. I hope that this suggested arrangement is acceptable to the company. Once again, thank you for your support.	**Heading** Provides the handwritten initials **Body** Introduction states the purpose clearly and directly Body expresses gratitude and gives reasons Conclusion builds goodwill

4. A proposal memo.

CONTACT COMPUTER GRAPHICS
MEMORANDUM

To: S M Chan, General Manager
From: Samantha Ng, Office Manager
Date: 5 April 2018
Subject: Purchase of a Microwave Oven

1. Introduction
At the monthly staff meeting on Monday, 2 April 2018, you requested information about the possible purchase of a microwave oven. I would now like to present these details. <!-- Subject describes proposal content -->

2. Background
Since the move to the new office in Kowloon Bay, staff have difficulty in finding a nearby place to buy lunch. <!-- States the main point -->

3. Advantages
Providing a microwave oven in the pantry would enable staff to bring in their own lunchboxes and reheat their food. Also, staff members are less likely to return to work late after lunch. <!-- Details relevant to the proposal -->

4. Staff Opinion
A survey found that staff would like to use the microwave oven. <!-- Uses headings and numbers to make reading easier -->

5. Cost
Details of suitable models are given below:

Brand	Model	Price
Philip	M903	$2 800
Sharpe	R-3R29	$2 600
Sonny	6145 X	$2 400

6. Request
If this meets with your approval, we would appreciate it if you could authorize up to $3 000 for the purchase of the microwave oven. <!-- Calls for action. Makes a request -->

Samantha Ng

Samantha Ng

5. A memo report.

806-A Manitoba Avenue
Selkirk, Manitoba R1A 2H4
Toll Free: 800-876-5831
Phone: 204-482-3717
Fax: 204-482-3799

Project Update Memo

Date: November 12th, 2017
To: RRPD Board
Cc: Kristi Lewis Tyran
Subject: RRPD Development Plan Update
Project update memo #5

RRPD Development Plan Update Project Component			
Component 1	**Component 2**	**Component 3**	**Component 4**
Project Start-up	Background Research	Update Development Plan	Adoption of Development plan
May – June 2017	*July – November 2017*	*December – February 2017/2018*	*March – April 2018*

Reporting period: August 4th — September 5th 2017
Current stage of project: Component 2 – Background Research

Here is a summary of my project so far:
Past Month Accomplishments:
• Continued with research and analysis related to Component 2 (Background Research) of the project, specifically for the drafting of a background report.
• Completed initial discussion with RRPD member municipalities.
• Draft of Supply and Demand Market Analysis completed by Stevenson Advisors Note: RRPD is currently reviewing the draft. A final draft will be provided to the RRPD Board at a future meeting.

Other notes:
• A project member has resigned from RRPD to pursue another career opportunity. His last day with the RRPD is September 8, 2017. This will have a negative impact on the project time-line, but the extent of the impact is unknown at this time.

Next Month Tasks:
• Continue with research and analysis related to Component 2, compile data, and complete a background report.
• Contact Joe Smith to get information about the tasks. Set up a meeting for next month.

Thank you for the opportunity to work with you. Please let me know if there are any updates or changes I need to make to my plan.

6. A meeting memo.

Memorandum of Meeting

Date: 11/22/04
Date of Meeting: 10/18/04
Time: 5:30 p.m.
Location: Georgetown CHEER Center
Type: Georgetown Area Working Group Meeting #5
Attendance: See Attached

The following is a summary of the discussion at the Working Group meeting:

• The meeting was called to order at 5:45 p.m. by Mr. Robert Kramer.

• Bob thanked those Working Group members in attendance for coming. He indicated that this evening's meeting was going to be low-tech, no Power Point Presentation, emphasis on Working Group members reviewing the plans for the upcoming Public Workshops and providing feedback on how the preliminary alternatives should be presented.

• Bob reviewed the agenda, which was included in the Working Groups hand-out materials and reiterated the emphasis for this evening's meeting. Bob then introduced Monroe Hite, III, DelDOT's Project Manager for the US 113 N/S Study to continue the meeting.

• Monroe welcomed everyone, emphasized the importance of going over the changes to the alternatives from the previous meeting and the Working Group being comfortable with those changes. Monroe then indicated that the Public Workshop for the Georgetown Area would be held on November the 9th in the CHEER Center from 4 p.m. to 7 p.m..

• Monroe then reviewed a summary of the comments generated by the Working Group at their last meeting on September 30th.

• Joe reviewed the minor changes to the Eastern Bypass options then introduced Mr. Jeff Riegner to review the changes made to the On-alignment and Western Bypass options.

• Jeff reviewed the changes to the On-alignment and Western Bypass options, including the reduction of the number of On-alignment Options from four to two. He then reviewed the traffic movement graphic and indicated that additional work over the next couple of months regarding traffic would be presented in the same format at the next Working Group meeting. Finally, he reviewed the Impacts Matrix, which was also included in their hand-out.

• Bob then opened the floor for comments / thoughts, in general, regarding things that had occurred to any of the Working Group members since the last meeting.

• David Pedersen discussed a modified beltway concept that was the result of the conversations in the previous breakout session that he was involved in at the last Working Group meeting. He indicated that it was important that, at the next Public Workshop, the public be made aware that the options are not either / or but that there is the ability to mix and match and combine solutions to develop the ultimate solution.

The meeting adjourned at 8:30 p.m..

IV Writing skills

Like most business correspondence, memos need to be short and direct, easy to read and understand. Memo readers often need quickly grasp the content and significance of the memo. They may:

- skim the entire memo for its key points and a few details they're interested in
- read only the executive summary
- read the entire document for the details that support its major claims or recommendations

This means that in writing a business memo, you should think carefully what you want to say and how to structure your memo to make reading easier for the readers.

Presenting the main point first

Because the reader is not likely to read the memo closely, most memos often begin with a statement of the problem or a found solution. You should begin your memo with one or two brief sentences that quickly **summarize the purpose of the memo or state the main point**.

- If the purpose is to ask someone to do something, that request should be in the first sentence.

  e.g. I respectfully request an extension of my time limit for travel and transportation to my home of selection.

- If the purpose is to inform the reader about the status of work in progress, this purpose should be the first sentence.

  e.g. This is to inform you about the work status of our department until the end of November.

- If the memo's purpose is to announce something, the gist of the announcement should be in the first sentence.

  e.g. I'm delighted to tell you that the Executive Council has approved your committee's recommendation concerning a company childcare center.

- If the purpose is to report something, the first paragraph should summarize the report and the rest of the memo should elaborate.

  e.g. In response to your request, I have investigated the delays in processing commercial loan applications over the past three months. The following is a summary of my findings and several recommendations on how to improve the current processing timeframe and put in place processes to avoid these problems in the future.

Offering brief well-organized paragraphs

The body paragraphs of a memo discuss and explain the subject logically. To communicate your ideas clearly, you should decide how to address needs and concerns of the readers, and organize your thoughts using a carefully chosen structure. Different types of memos use different structures. For example,

Informational memo

① Introduction: Provide main idea or state the issue; ② Discussion: Expand on the details; ③ Conclusion: Outline the action required.

Proposal memo

① State reason for writing; ② Outline the present situation; ③ State the writer's proposal; ④ Describe benefits, feasibility, or advantage(s); ⑤ Mention and diffuse disadvantages or obstacles; ⑥ End with a call to action.

Problem-solving memo

① State the problem; ② Explain or analyze the problem; ③ Discuss the solutions; ④ Make recommendations or explain the actions taken or to be taken for solving the problem.

Memo report

① Introduction / Problem statement / Situation; ② Body: Findings; ③ Recommendations; ④ Conclusion.

Task 3. Read the following memo messages. Identify the function of each numbered paragraph. Then rearrange the order of the paragraphs according the memo structure discussed above.

(1) An announcement memo (informational memo)

① We will offer four sessions: Sept.14, Sept.18, Sept.21, and Sept.28. Each session is from 4 to 6 p.m.. _____

② If you would like to register, please complete the attached form and return it to me before Monday, Sept.10. _____

③ The new scheduling software has just been installed and there will be in-house training for it. _____

(2) A proposal memo

① A duplex printing policy would allow the company to save considerable money by printing on both sides where possible. We should show employees how to set printer options to print on both sides and communicate the new policy requiring employees to use duplex printing wherever applicable. _____

② Cost savings would result from using less paper, fewer paper clips and staples, and less postage on larger mailouts. Duplex printing would reduce the following costs: paper ($250 / month), supplies ($25 / month), and postage ($15 / month). Duplex printing also supports the company's green initiatives to reduce waste.

③ The following is a brief cost saving proposal you requested on August 16. This proposal expresses the need for implementing a duplex printing policy.

④ The time associated with communicating the new policy to employees (is approximately 1 hour per employee). Additional months of use would offset the costs associated with this hour of lost productivity. In addition, there will be the resistance of employees to change and follow the new procedures. While there will always be those resistant to change initially, this is not a difficult adjustment to make.

⑤ Our current practice is all prints generated for employee use or customer mailouts require a separate piece of paper for each page of the document.

⑥ I look forward to hearing your ideas about my proposal.

Using format features to increase your memo's readability

A variety of formatting features can help you structure the memo and clarify your points.

1. Divide a memo into sections to guide readers to the information they're seeking. The order of the sections must be logical to develop meaning as a well-written essay.

2. Use bolded headings for sections to help the reader locate information of interest more quickly. Headings are more prevalent in memos than in letters.

- Headings should be parallel with each other.
- Headings should be specific and clear to allow the reader some idea of the content of the whole memo.

Examples of headings:
- *Benefits of Telecommuting*
- *The Influence of Technology on Telecommuting*
- *Action Needed to Implement Change*

3. Use numbers, bullets, tables and white space to guide the eyes of the reader. These format features can signal structure and make the information scannable.

Task 4. In the following memo, the headings are missing, and the bullet points have been removed from lists. For each paragraph choose an appropriate heading

from the box below and add it before the paragraph. Then, decide where you could put in bullets to make the document easier to read.

Advantages Background Purpose Suggestions Request

Memorandum

To: Sandra Lai, Manager
From: Hugo Tsang, Staff Liaison Committee
Date: 5 April 2018
Subject: Smoking in the office building

_____(1):
The Staff Liaison Committee would like to draw your attention to the issue of smoking in the office building.

_____(2):
A number of staff have reported persistent respiratory illnesses while others believe that cigarette smoke in the company's offices is unpleasant. Recently the Staff Committee discussed this issue and voted by a majority of 19 to 18 to propose banning cigarette smoking in the company's offices.

_____(3):
The staff in favour of banning smoking believe that the overall comfort and health of staff would improve if this change were to happen. This could reduce illness and staff absenteeism and ultimately increase productivity.

_____(4):
The Staff Liaison Committee would like you to consider this issue and the possibility of banning smoking in the company's offices.

_____(5):
To reduce indoor smoking, we have suggested to construct indoor smoking areas for smokers and allow smoking only in the designated areas. In the meantime, employees and visitors can be permitted to use e-cigarettes and other smokeless tobacco products at work.

V Exercises and Practice

Task 5. Write out the meanings of the abbreviations or acronyms in the following memos.

Unit 7 Professional Memos

1	2
Date: Current date From: Sarah Jones, Office Manager To: All managers CC: Yang, PA Subject: Meeting tomorrow FYI: The Head of HR is arriving tomorrow morning to present new appraisal procedures. ETA 9.00! Please be ready. (Yang, can you contact catering about refreshments?) BW	From: J Smith, Managing Director To: W Steffen, Project Manger BCC: Chief Executive Officer Subject: Progress on installation Date: 10/04/2011 Re the installation at the Ede site, we need an update ASAP on all the points discussed last week: N.B. The Board Meeting is to be held on October 15 (T.B.C). Can you come? Please RSVP to Susan Smith.

CC _____ ETA _____ ASAP _____
PA _____ BW _____ NB _____
HR _____ BCC _____ TBC _____
FYI _____ Re _____ RSVP _____

Writing a short memo

Task 6. Short memos are appropriate when making internal requests or announcements. Write a one-paragraph memo (40~60 words) for the following situations. Write a suitable heading and make the memo concise and easy to read. Refer to the useful phrases in the table below.

Providing routine information	Announcing a meeting or event	Requesting
• This is to inform / remind you that… • I would like to … • The following is … / Below are… • The purpose of this memo is to inform / remind you of… • Please note that…/ Please be aware… • In response to your request, I have…	• The quarterly meeting will be held on…at… • This year's…has been arranged • Please plan to meet at… • Please confirm your attendance by…by calling… • Please let me know by Friday whether…	• Please consider… / report… • I would like to… / I need to… • We kindly request… • Could you provide me with…? • Please take a couple of minutes to fill out the survey and return it by... • Thank you for your cooperation.
Announcing a company policy	**Proposing / Recommending**	**Internal report**
• Starting January 1, we are announcing a new policy. • Effective March 1, you will… • The new policy will take effect on… • This policy will be strictly enforced to make sure… • We invite your feedback. • You are welcome to suggest.	• As you requested, I have investigated / examined / studied … • It is recommended that…/ I recommend • Based on my research, I recommend / suggest that… • This will enable us to…	• The purpose of this report is to… • In this report I will review / offer recommendations for… • The following report presents… • At your request, we conducted… • To let you know the status of … • To update you on the progress of… • In summary, it can be stated / concluded that…

(1) You are Jeff Joyner, the Office Manager. You need to inform all staff of the annual company picnic. Invite them and their immediate family members to the picnic and ask them to reply by May 1, 2017.

```
                              MEMO
Date:
From:
To:
Subject:
```

(2) You are Anna Kapoor, the customer service representative. Mr. John Smith, the Customer Service Manager, has asked you to analyze the customer complaints received and report the results of your study. Write a memo in response to his request. You have attached a short report to the memo. Copy the memo to Jacob Kell, Marketing Manager.

```
                              MEMO
Date:
From:
To:
Subject:
```

(3) You are Aida Nolan. Send all employees a memo to announce a change in company policy. The company will stop using the old form of incident reports and introduce a new incident report protocol starting from January 1.

```
                              MEMO
Date:
From:
To:
Subject:
```

(4) Write a memo to all staff reminding them of two recycling containers in the office. Ask them to use bins to recycle waste properly (The blue one for bottles and cans. The red one for paper products.).

MEMO

Date:
From:
To:
Subject:

Writing a longer memo / memo report

Task 7. The following memo report outlines an investigation into processing delays in commercial loan applications. Complete the report by providing suitable headings and translating the expressions in the brackets from Chinese to English.

To: Margaret Curzon, Branch Manger
From: Jeffrey Blake, Loan Manager
Date: 30 September 2011
Subject: Investigation into processing delays in commercial loan applications

1. Introduction

_____ (① 应您的要求，我调查了) the delays in processing commercial loan applications over the past three months. _____
_____ (② 以下是我的调查结果、结论和建议) on how to improve the current processing timeframe and put in place processes to avoid these problems in the future.

2. _____

2.1 Processing time
The average processing time for a commercial loan application has slipped for the third consecutive month. It now takes approximately six weeks for our customers to get an answer on their loan application. This is more than two weeks longer than our advertised four-week turnaround time and longer than the turnaround time of most our competitors. _____(③ 造成下滑的原因包括) an increase in the number of loans currently being processed, an ongoing problem with the online loan approval system and the impact of staff leave schedules due to mid-year school holidays.

2.2 Commercial loans processed
The total number of commercial loans processed has continued to increase over the past 12 months. .During the past three months, these increases have been significant. _____
_____ (④ 以下是本季度贷款活动一览表).

(Continued)

Month	Total No. of loans initiated	Loan amount
June 2011	50	$350 000
July 2011	68	$598 000
August 2011	86	$843 000

2.3 Staff shortages

The last three months has seen an increased demand for annual leave by key loans staff. This, in addition to two senior staff taking extended long service leave plus one unexpected extended period of sick leave for a member of the conveyancing team, has meant increased workload for the whole section.

…

3. _____
_____(⑤正如本报告所概述), processing of loans is currently two weeks behind our advertised four-week turnaround on loan applications for several reasons beyond our control. Unfortunately, _____.
_____(⑥ 这对我们的业务有很 大的影响) with many customers choosing to apply to our competitors rather than wait. In short, the bank is losing important business due to these delays.

4. _____
_____.
(⑦ 根据我的研究，建议采取以下短期行动和长期行动).
(1) Immediately employ an additional loans officer to ease the burden on the department.
(2) Ensure that all staff leave is staggered during the end of financial year period.
(3) Advertise an immediate reduction in loan application fees until the backlog of applications has been processed.
_____(⑧ 我非常乐意与您讨论这些建议). If you are happy to approve recommendation 1, I will begin recruiting this additional staff member immediately.

Task 8. Look at these diagrams which are the result of a survey into current employee satisfaction with Lloyds' catering service. Refer to the memo report in Task 8 and complete the outline of a memo report based on the diagrams. Then expand the memo outline into a full memo report by using the expressions provided in the box.

☞ See Situation 4 in Assignments Section for the background of the memo report.

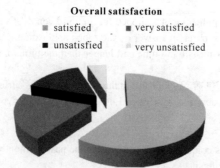
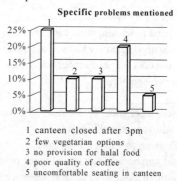

(Source: Hill David A, 2015, Life Advanced. Business Writing Worksheets, http://www.englishtips.org/…life-advanced-business-writing-worksheets.html)

Unit 7 Professional Memos

Outline	Useful expressions

1. Introduction
   Statement of the problem / purpose
   _____
2. _____
   2.1 _____
   2.2 _____
3. Conclusion
   _____
   _____
4. _____
   _____
	This report reviews / investigates …
	Its findings are based on …
	It was found that…
	It is worth noting that…
	Key areas which were…include the following:
	In general, … is considered…
	However, it can be concluded that…
	In short, …
	I recommend that we should take the following steps:
	…should be…
	  give priority to… / ensure that… / discuss….

Assignments

1. Write effective memos for the situations below. Send your message to each member of your group members.

Situation 1

You will need to inform the department staff about the decisions made at the meeting. You will award employees special annual bonus leave (additional 5 days) for outstanding performance. You ask them to attend the meeting next week to discuss the final list of employees eligible for the bonus.

Situation 2

As the HR Director, you want to ask the NIH Training Center to organize two interviewing skills training sessions for all associate recruiters. Write a memo to your assistant Linda asking her to contact the training center to make arraignments. Tell her there will be 18 participants for the training session. The suggested time are the weekends of October 3 and 10.

Situation 3

You are the manager of a small language school. The school canteen is going to be renovated in the next few months. You would like your staff to offer suggestions for redesigning the canteen. You plan to have a suggestion box so staff can contribute their ideas.

Situation 4

On April 3, the Personnel Department of Lloyds Inc. commissioned you to survey the overall satisfaction with the company's catering service among current employees. You interviewed one hundred employees (about 10% of the current workforce) asking them to comment on aspects of current practice and offer suggestions. Write a memo report to your Personnel Manager Stewart Jensen to summarize the result of your survey. Refer to Task 9 for more details.

2. Check and evaluate business memos.

Use the following checklist to revise your memos. Exchange your memo with your partner. Evaluate your partner's memo, pointing out its strengths and weaknesses.

Memo Writing Checklist

Heading
• Labels the document as a Memo or Memorandum.
• Includes To, From, Date, and Subject.
• The subject line forecasts the memo's contents
• Initials after your name in the "From" line (if it is a hardcopy memo).

Body
• The first sentence / paragraph of the memo states the purpose or raises the problem.
• The body provides all relevant, concise facts or important background information.
• The last sentence or paragraph states the expected action, make recommendations or ends the memo on a positive note.

Format & Style
• The memo is written in the proper format.
• Headings, lists, charts, or tables appear whenever needed.
• The writing style is clear, concise, exact, and appropriate.
• Keep paragraphs short and to the point.
• There are no spelling, grammatical or punctuation errors.

Comments
Anything that could be improved?

Anything that you particularly like?

Answer Key

Unit 1

Task 11

1. (3) (2) (1) 2. (2) (1) (3) 3. (1) (3) (2)

Task 12

(1) with, in, for, in (2) in, with, in, to

(3) to, as, in / at (4) to, with

(5) with (6) of (7) in (8) to

(9) at (10) for (11) about (12) for

Task 14

(1) Expected, Minor, Overall

(2) Master, Bachelor

(3) Concentration, Rank

(4) Thesis, double

(5) Relevant courses, Senior Project

Task 15

Research / Technical

(1) create (2) Conduct (3) Developed

(4) analyzed (5) Resolved

(6) Provide (7) Authored

Management / Leadership / Supervision

(1) delegated (2) manage (3) Coordinate

(4) Organized (5) Motivated (6) Initiated

Communication / People / Writing

(1) maintained (2) Communicated

(3) promote (4) Negotiated (5) Presented

Supporting / Helping

(1) Collaborate (2) Assisted (3) Participate

Achievements / Results / Recognition

(1) exceeding (2) Increased (3) Achieved

(4) Earned (5) Won (6) Received (7) Ranked

(8) resulted in (9) Outperformed

Task 16

(1) Managed $3-4 million budget projects and achieved schedule goals.

(2) Tested web applications, mobile apps, networks, hardware, and stand-alone applications with a 100% accuracy.

(3) Collaborated with other members of college speech and debate team that won Top Award in IPDA Public Debate Contest three years in a row.

(4) Supervised / Managed / Led a top performing team of 10 professionals, motivating the team to exceed sales goals by over $2 million each year/reaching annual goals while promoting effective customer service.

(5) Organized campus activities including athletic events and signing contest for over 300 freshmen, and increased student engagement by 30% through flyers, posters, targeted emails and social networking websites.

Task 17

Work Experience

2016 – Present Software Engineer I-Solution

• Maintain and develop high quality software systems for clients.

• Utilize software engineering tools to perform technical root cause analysis.

2013 – 2015 System Analyst ABC Company

• Performed feasibility studies, data modeling and analysis service.

• Implemented decision support system for the Real Estate Division.

Internship

2015 – 2017   Research Intern   Washington Institute for Near East Policy

• Collaborated with 3 interns to collect data and perform research.

• Authored reports for interviews and publications on subjects including Arab Politics, NGOs in Egypt and Tunisia.

• Monitored key regional political developments such as the rise of ISIS.

Activities

2017 – Present   Captain

Salisbury University soccer team.

• Motivate 20 players and coordinate all indoor practices as well as scheduling all weight room activities.

• Set a standard of excellence through hard work and dedication.

Task 20

(1) Heading

Li Ming

No 10, Xitucheng Road, Haidian District, Beijing, PRC, 100876

Cell:134×××××××

E-mail: Ming-Li@163.com

(2) Education

Master of Science in Communication Engineering   June 2015
Beijing University of Posts and Telecommunication
Main Courses:
Communication Theory, Signal and System, Wavelet Analysis, C++ Language
Bachelor of Science in Communication Engineering   June 2012
Harbin Engineering University

(3) Experience

RELATED EXPERIENCE
Salesperson   *Walmart, Shenzhen*
September 2014 to present
• Build merchandise displays
• Manage and tracked inventory
• Maintain customer relations
Shift Supervisor   *Star Coffee Shop, Shenzhen*
May 2013 to Aug. 2014
• Trained 5 new employees
• Handled total sales

(4) Honors and awards

First-class Scholarship
Spring 2014, Fall 2015
Merit Student Award
December 2009
1st Place in National Undergraduate Electronic Design Contest in Liaoning Province
July 2011

(5) Activities

Network Assistant (volunteer) – Phoenix Garden
September 2001– May 2002.
• Assembled 20 computers for new computer laboratory, loaded software on each one, and networked them.

(6) Skills

Language skills
CET-6, Fluent in English / Intermediate proficiency in English
Computer skills
Microsoft Word, Excel, and PowerPoint
C, C++, Java, Linux, Dreamweaver, Adobe Photoshop

Unit 2

Task 6

Generic opener	(2) (3)
Attention-grabbing opener	Start with company facts (5)
	Highlight your impressive skills or accomplishments (4)
	Convey enthusiasm or passion (6)
	Mention a personal referral (1)

Task 8

(1) — (c);(2) — (d);(3) — (a); (4) — (b)

Task 9

(1) Emphasize the candidates potential value to the organization.

(2) Demonstrate the candidates commitment and value.

(4) Show the candidates enthusiasm and confidence.

(5) Review the candidates key selling points.

Task 10

(2) too short, informal, rude

(3) negative, humble

(5) arrogant, bloated self-importance

(6) not enthusiastic, not confident

(7) humble

Task 11

(1) I am writing to apply for the Senior Marketing Officer position posted on CareerTimes.com on 23 September 2016.

(2) Please accept my resume in consideration for your sales manager position.

(3) I would like to express my strong interest in the position of Research Fellow in Applied Health Research which was advertised on jobs.ac.uk.

(4) I am writing to you in response to your advertisement for a Legal Assistant specializing in Criminal Law, which appeared in the Seattle Times on June 15.

Task 12

(1) As an engineer with a bachelor's degree in both computer science and software engineering, respectively, I am excited to apply for the opening for a computer software engineer at XYZ.

(2) With a proven record in delivering projects ahead of time and under budget, I am confident that I can make an immediate contribution to the success of your company.

(3) My academic training in strategic analysis coupled with demonstrated management skills, as evidenced by my leadership role at Youthbuild, would enable me to expand your company's growth and work towards a more sustainable future.

Task 13

(1) During my 2012 summer internship / I acted as a liaison / not only gained more insights into , but also improved my ability to…

(2) This past summer, I served as the principal investigator / compelling me to become expertly familiar with…

(3) the knowledge I have acquired / These courses have provided me with understanding / sharpened my analytical skills…

(4) Beyond the classroom, I have taken an active role in campus activities / These leadership roles have allowed me to interact with a diverse group of people, demonstrating my organizational and communication skills.

(5) This experience has made me aware of the importance of cross-cultural learning and global understanding.

(6) In this role, I gained valuable experience in. / This experience has given me a strong foundation.

Task 14

in, for, for, with, in, to, on, to, with, on, with, for, at, at

Unit 3

Task 5

A) 4132　B) 3214

Task 7

S, T, A, R

Task 9

1. (1) in, past, apply, prepared, Award, reinforced
   (2) been working, current, known for, miss, appreciates, passionate
   (3) majoring, focused, demonstrated, gained
2. (1) fit, mix　(2) emphasizes, previous, growth
3. (1) learn　(2) ethic, standard, bonus
4. (1) Sometimes, However, improved, on
   (2) trouble, Luckily, Since, learnt
5. (1) aligns, fit, skilled
   (2) match, recent, responsible, required, commitment
6. (1) impressed, increase　(2) commitment, reputation
7. (1) growing, responsibilities
   (2) opportunity, Once

Task 10

(1) I've known about your company for a long time.

(2) I'm really honored that you're considering me.

(3) My most valuable skill for this position is my fluency in French.

(4) in school I always scored ahead of the curve.

(5) With ten years of experience and a master's degree, I am a perfect match for the position.

(6) I started as an entry-level engineer and worked my way up to a senior engineer.

(7) My coworkers were impressed with my efficiency.

(8) I think one of my best qualities is my dependability.

(9) I am willing to go the extra mile to get the job done on time.

(10) When can I expect to hear from you? / When can I have your decision?

Unit 4

Task 3

Letter: More formal / Letterhead & address, date, return address, reader's address, salutation, complimentary close, and signature.

Email: Internal and external / Less formal / Short.

Memo: Internal only / Usually informal, sometimes formal / From, To, Date, Subject, message / Usually short, sometimes long(memo report).

Task 5

(1) enthusiastic, confident

(2) appreciative, regretful

(3) enthusiastic, thankful

(4) direct

(5) polite, indirect

(6) humble, appreciative to the person for being a client, confident that the mistake will be remedied

(7) warm and friendly

(8) firm but courteous

Task 6

(1) too informal　(2) too direct, impolite

(5) too formal　(6) too direct, impolite

(7) impolite, critical

Task 10

(1) Enclosed is… / I've enclosed…

(2) As requested / As you request

(3) Please note

(4) This is to tell you that we received your cheque / your payment has been received

Task 11

Prior to the event = before

In spite of the fact that = Although

At this point in time = now

Basic fundamentals = fundamentals

Subsequent to = after

In the year of 2018 = in 2018

In the event that = if

Merge together = merger

In view of the fact that = because

Mutual cooperation = cooperation

Answer Key

Until such time as = until

Long in length = long

Because of the fact that = because

give assistance to = help

Really excellent = excellent

Have a discussion = discuss

Task 12

(1) Because many of the words in this sentence are unnecessary, we should edit it.

(2) We have enclosed a report showing further details of construction on page four. / Page four of the enclosed report shows further construction details.

(3) If we must go out to shop with them, we should first go to the bank because I am out of cash.

(4) Twenty-five students have already expressed a desire to attend the program next summer. They should / It is important for them gain the most by the government grant.

(5) Mr. Stevens, our Chief Financial Officer, won his lawsuit.

Task 13

(1) Please remember to clean your work area before you leave each day.

(2) Positive words are preferable in your messages / Do not use negative words in your messages.

(3) The drive-through banking service is available after 9 a.m..

(4) Goods in good condition will be exchanged.

Task 14

(1) You will receive two uniforms next Monday morning.

(2) You will get a 2 percent discount if the bill is paid by the 10th of the month.

(3) A number of errors have been made in the paper / The paper includes a number of proofreading errors.

(4) You'll become a better communicator by taking our training courses.

Unit 5

Task 3

Message 1: (3) (2) (4) (1)   Message 2: (3) (1) (4) (2)

Task 5

(1) Thank you for your suggestion that that we hire an additional secretary. I agree that at times our present staff seems overwhelmed by the work load. Unfortunately, I would not consider new staff at this time. I have kept a copy of your letter and will talk to them again in six months or so.

(2) Please complete the enclosed advertisement contract and return it to us by July 1, 19×× so that you can renew your advertisement space./ Please complete and return the enclosed contract by July 1, 19××. After this deadline, we will begin selling any unrenewed advertisement space to other clients, so I hope we hear from you before then.

(3) In your letter you ask for a good amount of information which I would like to help you locate. Because of my work commitments, however, I am going to be able to answer only a few of the questions.

(4) I am certainly open to suggestions and comments about specific aspects of this article, or any of your thoughts on additional areas that you think I should cover. I do want, however, to retain the basic theme of the article: the usability of the Victor microcomputer system.

Task 7

(1) attention

(2) in reply to, regarding / concerning, apologize, caused

(3) congratulations

(4) find out / inquire

(5) reference, would like to request

(6) inquiry, enclosed, inform

(7) Following / Further to, delighted

(8) express my gratitude, assure

Task 8

(1) We are glad to inform you that your proposal for the project has been reviewed and accepted. We would like to arrange a meeting with you to sign the agreement. We are eagerly looking forward to this project and are happy to have the opportunity to work with you.

(2) I am applying for the position of sales manager and would appreciate a letter of reference.

(3) I would like to invite you, on behalf of the organizing committee to be our keynote speaker and guest of honor at the upcoming 2017 International Disabled Children Research Conference. (I am delighted to extend our invitation to you to be…/ It is with great pleasure that I…)

(4) In reply to your inquiry of 20 May, / In response to your letter dated May 20, we enclose our latest catalogue.

(5) Further to our letter of September 10th, we can now confirm that all the spare parts you requested are available.

Task 9

(1) I am looking forward to attending the event. Thank you, for the invite, and I will make sure that I can give you my best.

(2) I kindly request you to grant the permission and reply in writing regarding the same. / I look forward to hearing from you. / Thank you for considering this request. / Thank you very much for your attention to this matter.

(3) Thank you for your contributions to the company. If you have any further questions, please get in contact with "contact name". My best wishes for success in your future endeavors. / We extend our best wishes to you and wish you luck in your future endeavors.

(4) Once again, I would like to express my thanks towards you for referring your friend to our services. Your effort is truly appreciated.

Task 10

(1) H,G   (2) A,C,E,J   (3) B,D,F,I

Task 11

(1) delighted   (2) convenient / suitable

(3) review   (4) concerning

(5) numerous   (6) assure

(7) ensure   (8) angry

(9) request   (10) inform, terminate

(11) enquire   (12) supply

(13) at your earliest convenience

(14) Furthermore

Task 12

(1) I would be grateful / I would appreciate (it) if you could …

(2) I am writing to enquire whether…

(3) I am writing to inform you…

(4) I apologise for the delay in replying.

(5) I / We apologise for the inconvenience.

(6) Please accept our / my sincere apologies.

(7) I would be delighted / pleased to…

(8) I / We regret to inform you that …

(9) Unfortunately, we are unable to…

(10) We very much appreciate your… / we're grateful for

(11) I / We wish to draw your attention to…

(12) I am writing to complain about…

(13) I am writing to express my dissatisfaction with…

(14) You may contact me by telephone at…

(15) we look forward to hearing from you.

(16) Please do not hesitate to contact me.

Task 13

Dear Mr. Lee,

I regret to inform you that I have to cancel the meeting that we had scheduled for Tuesday, January 18th at 10 a.m. An unexpected scheduling conflict has arisen and has caused me to have to cancel our appointment.

I am very much looking forward to meeting with you, however, and would like to find a mutually agreeable time when we can hold a rescheduled meeting. Would Tuesday, January 25th at 11 a.m. work for you? Please call or E-mail me to let me know.

I apologize for any inconvenience that this change might create. I look forward to seeing you in the near future.

Sincerely,

Mandy Baines

Unit 6

Task 3

Dear Stephen,

I hope you are well. It was great to hear from you–thank you for your time. I wonder if you might have time to review my progress report. It is due for submission on Wednesday, so I would really appreciate any comments that you could make before then. If you are too busy to have a look, that's fine. I realize that it is short notice.

Thank you in advance.

Have a good day.

Lin Feng

Task 4

(1) Complaint about Delay in Delivery of Order

(2) Marketing Coordinator interview follow up / John Smith Following Up on Marketing Coordinator Position

(3) Invitation: Educational Meeting, San Joaquin, June 5

(4) Apology for late work submission

(5) Get Together on 11th April

Task 5

Dear XYZ Project Team Member,

Welcome to XYZ Project. I look forward to working with each of you.

The XYZ Project will be starting soon. I will be heading up this project. I need to set some ground rules for project meetings.

Project Meeting Ground Rules:

1. Be on time for all team meetings.
2. Attend full duration of all team meetings unless a case of emergency.
3. Send the team leader your issues before the meeting.
4. Distribute the agenda before the meeting.
5. Inform the team leader if unable to complete work on time.

Once again, welcome to XYZ Project. Let me know if you have any questions.

Sincerely,

Laura

XYZ Project Team Lead

Task 6

(1) Please let us know your requirements.

(2) We regret to inform you that

(3) We would like to remind you that …

(4) I can assure you that …

(5) I would appreciate it if you could…

(6) It is necessary for me to …

(7) Thanks for your email.

(8) I'll deal with this.

(9) I'm really sorry for / about…

(10) As you requested, I have attached…

(11) Get in touch with me if you have questions

Task 7

1. I'd like you to / Could you send me the sales figures in the second quarter before Friday afternoon?

2. I was hoping / wondering if you would be interested in my suggestions about increasing sales in our region. I would be grateful if you could spare 20 minutes to meet with me.

3. Would it be possible for me to take Monday morning off because I have some personal issues to take care of. If approved, I would make up the time later in the week.

4. I would like to say that I have accepted another opportunity that closely aligns with my skills and career goals. After much thought, I regret to decline your offer. / Unfortunately, I will not be accepting the position and would like to withdraw my application for the job due to some personal reasons.

5. It seems to me that there are some mistakes in your invoice / you may have made some mistakes on the invoice.

Task 8

Hi Dave,

I hope that everything is OK over there. I just have a few questions about the Skipton Airport Project.

First, can you give me an update on where you are on the project? I was hoping you could explain what the current issues with the delivery system are and confirm when you expect them to be resolved.

Also, at the end of our last meeting I asked for a copy of the latest Project Report. I still haven't received one. Can you forward it to me?

Please get back to me with the information as soon as possible.

Thanks,

Ian

Task 10

asap: as soon as possible (Y)

Encl.: enclosure (Y)

Att.: attention (Y)

FYI: For your information (Y)

BTW: by the way (N)

tks: thanks (N)

FAQs: Frequently asked questions (Y)

Bcc: Blind carbon copy (Y)

c/o : care of (Y)

n/a: not applicable/available (Y)

PS: postscript (Y)

LOL: laugh out loud (N)

TTYL: talk to you later (N)

G2G: got yo go (N)

CU: see you L8R: later (N)

Task 11

Message 1

To: J.Green@personnel.CivilandCivic.com.

Cc: S_Clark@admin.CivilandCivic.com

Bcc:

Subject: Smoking ban

Message 2

To: john_doe@jones.com

Cc:

Bcc: mary_smith@jones.com, and sam_jones@jones.com.

Subject: Last year's sales

Task 12

(1) E   (2) C   (3) B   (4) D   (5) A

Task 13

(1) Please contact me if you need any help.

(2) I look forward to hearing from you.

(3) See you soon.

(4) Please send me a reply as soon as possible.

(5) For the confirmation of your attendance, please RSVP by August 7 to Annette in Human Resources at 555-1212.

Task 14

(1) B   (2) I   (3) N   (4) D   (5) C   (6) K

(7) M   (8) O   (9) L   (10) G   (11) H   (12) J

Task 15

(1) This is to inform you of / Please attend

Each of us should be prepared to give an update on our current projects

send it to me / contact by email.

Let me know / Please get back to me / Please reply as soon as possible if you can attend

(2) I confirm that I will be attending / This is to confirm / I would like to confirm

May I suggest two other topics for our meeting?

(3) Thank you for your invitation

scheduled

I will make sure that I have the report you requested prepared and ready to present at the said meeting

I look forward to seeing you

(4) I am pleased to receive your invitation

Unfortunately, due to I will not be able to attend the meeting

I apologise for any inconvenience this may cause

If you have further questions, please do not hesitate to contact me

(5) Thanks for getting back to me about the meeting

I appreciate

If you could reconsider attending the meeting, we'd all appreciate it

(6) I'm afraid that I can't make this Friday's meeting has just come up

I'm sorry for the short notice

Is there any chance we can move the meeting to next week

Let me know if that's OK for you.

(7) Thanks for letting me know

we've all agreed that we can move the meeting to a time and date which is more suitable for your schedule

(8) concerning

Please find minutes of the meeting attached to this email for your review of the event, please refer to the attached minutes of the meeting

regarding the content of the document

Task 16

Formal: 3,4,6,8,10,12   Informal: 1,2,5,7,9,11

Task 17

(1) We motivated staff by introducing lunch talks.

(2) The chairman concluded we needed to improve the system.

(3) We have several job openings in our R&D department.

(4) We are addressing our team's performance issues

(5) Despite our increasing advertising budget, sales have not improved.

(6) The company recognised that it needed better staff training, so they decided to recruit a Training Director.

(7) We didn't reply because we learned only yesterday that the report has been delayed.

Unit 7

Task 3

(1) ③ (Introduction)   ① (Discussion)
     ② (Conclusion)

(2) ③ (State the reasons for writing)
     ⑤ (Outline the present situation)
     ① (State the writer's proposal)
     ② (Describe benefits or advantages)
     ④ (Mention disadvantages or obstacles)
     ⑥ (End with a call to action)

Task 4

(1) Introduction, Situation

(2) Background

(3) Advantages

(4) Request

(5) Suggestion

To reduce indoor smoking, we have suggested to

- construct indoor smoking areas for smokers
- allow smoking only in the designated areas.
- permit employees and visitors to use e-cigarettes and other smokeless tobacco products at work.

Task 5

CC: carbon copy

PA: Personal Assistant

HR : Human Resources

FYI: for your information

ETA: estimated time of arrival

BW: best wishes

BCC : blind carbon copy

ASAP: as soon as possible

Re: regarding; on the subject of

NB: Nota Bene / Note well / Please note

TBC: To be confirmed

RSVP: Please reply

Task 7

① In response to your request, I have investigated

② The following is a summary of my findings, conclusion and recommendations

③ The reasons for this slippage include

④ The table below is a summary of this quarter's loan activity

⑤ As outlined in this report;

⑥ this is having significant effect on business,

⑦ Based on my study, I recommend the following short-term and long-term actions.

⑧ I would be happy to meet with you to discuss these recommendations.

Reference

[1] 窦卫霖. 跨文化商务交际 [M]. 2 版. 北京：高等教育出版社，2011.

[2] 菲利普·C. 科林. 成功职场英语写作 [M]. 8 版. 王雷，译. 北京：中国市场出版社，2010：139-143.

[3] 胡鹏. 简历：让你脱颖而出 [M]. 北京：机械工业出版社，2011.

[4] 肯·欧奎恩. 商务信函写作一本通 [M]. 高勤，译. 北京：人民邮电出版社，2013:184-187

[5] 叶红. 走进职场英语写作 [M]. 2 版. 北京：外语教学与研究出版社，2017:58-64.

[6] Donald H. Cunningham, Elizabeth O. Smith, Thomas E. Pearsall. 职场英语写作 [M]. 7 版. 北京：北京大学出版社，2011: 209, 219.

[7] George J. Searles. Workplace Communication: The Basics 职场英语写作实战速成 [M]. 5 版. 北京：清华大学出版社，1995：9, 38.

[8] Nick Brieger. Collins English for Business: Writing [M]. 北京：商务印书馆，2013:33-35.

[9] Colm Downes. Cambridge English for Job-hunting [M]. Cambridge University Press, 2008:20-28.

[10] Les Hanson, Darryl Hammond. Business Communication: Contexts and Controversies [M]. Pearson Education Canada, 2010:177-178.

[11] Richard Walsh. The Complete Job Search Book for College Students [M]. 3rd ed. Adams Media; 2007: 55-56, 78-83.

[12] Sharon J. Gerson, Steven M. Gerson. Workplace Writing: Planning, Packaging, and Perfecting Communication [M]. Pearson, 2009:46.

[13] Sherry J. Roberts. Fundamentals of Business Communication [M]. Goodheart-Willcox Publisher, 2012: 201-208.

[14] Shirley Taylor. Model Business Letters, Emails and Other Business Documents [M]. 7th ed. Financial Times / Prentice Hall, 2015:30-33, 44 -47.